40 Days of

Teshuvah

Unlocking the Mystery of
God's Prophetic Seasons and Cycles

40 Days of

Teshuvah

Unlocking the Mystery of
God's Prophetic Seasons and Cycles

Perry Stone, Jr.

WITH ADDITIONAL RESEARCH BY

Bill Cloud

Voice of Evangelism
Cleveland, TN

40 DAYS OF TESHUVAH:
Unlocking the Mystery of God's Prophetic Seasons and Cycles

Copyright © 2006 by Perry Stone, Jr.

ISBN 0-9785920-0-X

First Printing - August 2006

Unless otherwise indicated, Scripture quotations are from the New King James Version, © 1990, 1995 by Thomas Nelson Publishers, Nashville TN.

Cover design: Michael Dutton

Printed in the United States of America.

CONTENTS

Chapter One

Signs, Seasons and the Moon

"Sing aloud unto God our strength: make a joyful noise unto the God of Jacob. Take a psalm, and bring hither the timbrel, the pleasant harp with the psaltery. Blow up the trumpet in the new moon, **in the time appointed**, on our solemn feast day. For this was a statute for Israel, and a law of the God of Jacob." - Psalm 81:1-4 (KJV)

Most Christians are not familiar with the Hebraic concept of the Bible, this despite the fact that most Christians understand that Jesus, the Apostles, the Prophets and the majority of other notables in the Bible were of Hebrew descent. This ignorance of the Hebraic nature of Scripture had led to much misunderstanding and, consequently and unfortunately, a degree of misinterpretation of the Scripture. This misunderstanding has affected how we think, and how we think affects our outlook on life, our doctrinal beliefs and our view of prophecy.

One of the most glaring examples of this Scriptural ignorance is the "appointed times" of God. What makes this so interesting, and a bit puzzling I might add, is that the appointed times are one of the first things established at the beginning of Creation.

"Then God said, Let there be lights in the firmament of the heavens to divide the day from the night; and let them be for signs and seasons, and for days and years." (Genesis 1:14)

The word translated here as "seasons" is the Hebrew *moedim* or "appointed times." And so we understand that the heavenly luminaries - the sun, moon and stars - were placed in the cosmos in part to teach us of these appointed times of God. As you can see by what the psalmist declares in Psalm 81, the Hebrew people were well aware of these appointed times and conducted their lives in accordance with the specific seasons that God had ordained. The psalmist also makes it clear that these *moedim* were connected to the heavenly bodies, in this case, the moon.

Israel and the Lunar Cycle

The Hebrew word translated as "month" is *chodesh.* There are occasions when this same Hebrew word is translated as "moon. The Hebrew root word, *chadash*, means "to renew." Thus, the Hebraic view of a month is tied to the idea of something being "renewed." That "something" is the moon which renews itself every twenty-nine to thirty days. This cycle begins with what is called a "new moon" - known in Hebrew as *rosh chodesh* or "head of the month." Following this initial stage, this heavenly body will continue to "wax" greater until at the midpoint of the cycle - typically the fourteenth or fifteenth day - it will become full. From that point it will begin to wane until it disappears totally, thus starting the cycle over again.

That is the simple explanation of what happens during this cycle, but what does it mean? What is the spiritual significance? First, we should understand that the lunar cycle and particularly the new moon was of the utmost importance to Israel. In fact, every new moon was considered a Sabbath (the new moon of the seventh month is regarded as a "High Sabbath") and was acknowledged as such with feasting and presenting offerings.

"AT THE BEGINNING OF YOUR MONTHS (THE NEW MOON) YOU SHALL PRESENT A BURNT OFFERING TO THE LORD; TWO YOUNG BULLS, ONE RAM, AND SEVEN LAMBS IN THEIR FIRST YEAR, WITHOUT BLEMISH." (NUMBERS 28:11)

"THEN JONATHAN SAID TO DAVID, 'TOMORROW IS THE NEW MOON, AND YOU WILL BE MISSED, BECAUSE YOUR SEAT WILL BE EMPTY.' . . . AND WHEN THE NEW MOON HAD COME, THE KING SAT DOWN TO EAT THE FEAST."
(1 SAMUEL 20:18, 24)

Secondly we should note that the moon itself is a heavenly "body" incapable of generating its own light. By design it may only reflect the light of the sun. So then, there are times when this reflection can not be seen from Earth. When it is hidden from view, astronomers refer to this as a "new moon." Actually, the moon is still there but we can't see it because it is in a state called "conjunction."

Because the moon doesn't rotate on its axis as the earth does, the same side of the moon always faces the sun and the other side always faces away from the sun. This is why we have the "dark side of the moon." As the moon revolves around the earth, it will eventually move directly between the sun and the earth. The side of the moon that always faces away from the sun - the dark side - will be facing the earth. This factor, coupled with the fact that the overpowering glare of direct sunlight has the ability to conceal things from view - as when you are driving into the late afternoon sun - results in the moon being hidden from our eyes.

Again, this "conjunction" is what astronomers refer to as a "new moon," however, this is not what the Bible means by "new moon." In biblical days, after the moon disappeared, witnesses would wait and watch every night for the "renewing" of the moon - they knew that it would eventually reappear. Science tells us that after the moon is in conjunction, it typically exits that concealed state and reappears in the night sky after an average of 2.5 days. In other words, it renews itself - it is "born again - on the third day!

When it first reappears and we can once again see the light of the sun being reflected off of the face of the moon - because it can't produce its own light - the Bible refers to this renewal as the "new moon." Tradition has it that when two or more witnesses saw the new moon, they were to sound the shofar. They would then make this sighting known to the Sanhedrin who would then convey the news to the the High Priest. Through the High Priest, all of Israel would be alerted to the start of the new month. This information was crucial, because only through accurately establishing the months could Israel faithfully keep the "appointed times" of the Lord.

There are many lessons that we can learn from the lunar cycle, but I will relate just one primary lesson to you here. As I have already noted, the moon is representative of a "body." The rabbis have said that it represents Israel. Of course, God would not choose the sun to represent Israel because the sun doesn't need to be renewed - it just is. In fact, the very light we mistakenly refer to as "moonlight" isn't moonlight at all, but the light of the sun being reflected off of the face of the moon.

Because the moon does reflect the light of the Sun, it becomes obvious to us as Christians that this is a picture of us as well. To see it this way is not inaccurate and is not to dispute that the moon is representative of Israel. How can they both be right? Because we understand through the writings of Paul that, through Jesus Christ, you and I have been grafted into the family God calls Israel (Rom. 11).

When we consider Israel's connection to the lunar cycle please pay attention to the fact that, beginning with the new moon and continuing until the full moon, the world goes from dark to light. In other words, at the beginning of the cycle there is darkness but by the time we reach a full moon, there is sufficient light to see. Furthermore, after the brightness of the full moon the light begins to wane until there is complete darkness again.

With this in mind, consider that from Abraham to Solomon is fifteen generations corresponding to the first fifteen days of the lunar cycle. At the beginning, in Abraham's day, the glory that would become Israel was only a promise. This would be personified by the appearance of the new moon. But by the days of Solomon, the promise had become more of a reality. In Solomon's' day, Israel enjoyed great prosperity and peace, due mainly to the fact that the Presence of God dwelt among them in the Temple of the Lord. Thus, Solomon - the fifteenth from Abraham - corresponds to the full moon which occurs typically on the fifteenth day of the month.

His father, David, would have been the fourteenth from Abraham. Interestingly enough, the numerical equivalent of David as written in Hebrew is fourteen. Between David and his son Solomon, Israel enjoyed some of the greatest days of their history.

After Solomon though, the light began to wane until fifteen generations later, the light was extinguished. It was in that generation, in the days of King Zedekiah, that the Temple was destroyed and the

House of Judah was taken into Babylonian captivity.

Still, the story does not end there, because like the moon which is renewed again and again, Israel was destined to be restored back to her former glory. Thus, the prophet Hosea wrote that:

"COME, AND LET US RETURN TO THE LORD; FOR HE HAS TORN, BUT HE WILL HEAL US; HE HAS STRICKEN, BUT HE WILL BIND US UP. AFTER TWO DAYS HE WILL REVIVE US; ON THE THIRD DAY HE WILL RAISE US UP, THAT WE MAY LIVE IN HIS SIGHT." (HOSEA 6:1-2)

Keeping in mind that the new moon typically occurs on the third day after being hidden for the previous two days, we see that Hosea's prophecy speaks in concert with the lunar cycle. After two days, Israel (which includes those of us who are followers of Jesus the Messiah) will return to the Lord after being in darkness. On the third day they will be "raised up" - revived, renewed - so that they may live in His sight.

As far as Christians are concerned, for two thousand years, we have lived in darkness when it comes to understanding God's ways and methods of performing His Will. By that I mean, by and large we have not recognized His "appointed times" and how He established them in the Hebrew Scriptures and, more importantly, how the Messiah fulfilled them and how He even alluded to them in the Gospels. For instance, on the night before His death - at Passover, one of the "appointed times" - Jesus took the third cup of the Passover meal and said something very interesting.

"LIKEWISE, HE ALSO TOOK THE CUP AFTER SUPPER, SAYING, 'THIS CUP IS THE NEW COVENANT IN MY BLOOD, WHICH IS SHED FOR YOU.' " (LUKE 22:20)

To most Christians, this verse seems to say that the reason Jesus came to earth was to make a brand new covenant with us through His death. In other words, our perception of "new" is that it is something that has not been seen or used before. The reality is not exactly what we have perceived. To understand what He actually meant can only be understood by looking at it through the Hebrew Scriptures and understanding God's appointed times.

When Jesus announced the offering of the "new covenant in My blood," we understand He was not speaking in English but In Hebrew. In that language Jesus would have said *"brit chadashah b'dami"* - literally rendered, **"renewed** covenant in my blood." Please notice the word *chadashah* or "renewed." This is derived from the same root - *chadash* - that gives birth to the word *chodesh*, interpreted as "month" and sometimes as "moon."

Considering what we now know about the lunar cycle, we are to understand that the Messiah was **renewing** a covenant that had already been initiated but which had also been "lost" or "hidden." That this is the case can be better perceived when we understand that this "renewed covenant" was prophesied of by the prophet Jeremiah.

"BEHOLD, THE DAYS ARE COMING, SAYS THE LORD, WHEN I WILL MAKE A NEW COVENANT WITH THE HOUSE OF ISRAEL AND WITH THE HOUSE OF JUDAH - NOT ACCORDING TO THE COVENANT THAT I MADE WITH THEIR FATHERS IN THE DAY THAT I TOOK THEM BY THE HAND TO LEAD THEM OUT OF THE LAND OF EGYPT; MY COVENANT WHICH THEY BROKE, THOUGH I WAS A HUSBAND TO THEM, SAYS THE LORD. BUT THIS IS THE COVENANT THAT I WILL MAKE WITH THE HOUSE OF ISRAEL AFTER THOSE DAYS, SAYS THE LORD. I WILL PUT MY LAW IN THEIR MINDS, AND WRITE IT ON THEIR HEARTS, AND I WILL BE THEIR GOD AND THEY SHALL BE MY PEOPLE."
(JEREMIAH 31:31-33)

In the above passage, the word translated as "new" is *chadashah*, and so it should be rendered as "renewed." The Lord makes it clear through Jeremiah that the covenant He refers to has been presented before and then broken. The renewal of this covenant would successfully accomplish results not attained by the previous covenant. By the words of Jesus we understand that the difference in the covenant would be that its confirmation and atonement would not be accomplished with the blood of bulls or goats (Heb. 9:12) but by the blood of Messiah, the Son of God, who Himself would be "renewed" or **resurrected** on the third day - just like the moon on *Rosh Chodesh*!

Now, here we are two thousand years later and some Christians are just now realizing the depth of this and its relationship to God's appointed times. Nevertheless, it seems that God's cycles actually predicted this failure to understand completely and, more importantly, predicted when we would begin to "see the light." In other words, if it has been two thousand years since the Messiah was crucified, buried and resurrected, then it has actually been two days.

"BELOVED, DO NOT FORGET THIS ONE THING, THAT WITH THE LORD ONE DAY IS AS A THOUSAND YEARS, AND A THOUSAND YEARS AS ONE DAY." (2 PETER 3:8)

Understanding that two days have passed since the Messiah established the "Renewed Covenant" - (in Hebrew, *Brit Chadashah*) - then we should also understand that we are on the threshold of the third day. Through the lessons of the lunar cycle, and specifically the new moon, we are to understand that, on the third day, what has been hidden will reappear. When that happens, witnesses to this event are to sound the alarm so that all of God's people will understand what is about to happen. We all need to be aware that things new are about to take place, We all need to be awakened to the fact that God wants to show us something that we have not seen up until this point.

To put it another way, we must understand the significance of the lunar cycle, and especially the "new moon," if we are to more fully understand the importance and extent of all God's appointed times. Though the moon "seems" to disappear, it is actually being renewed consistently. Understanding this, we can better appreciate that God's way of doing things with and for His people is always **renewal** not reinvention. If we can grasp the significance of the lunar cycle, then we have a solid foundation upon which to build the revelations inherent in all the other God-appointed times.

TWO OR MORE WITNESSES

In Psalm 81, the writer admonishes Israel to blow the shofar - the Biblical trumpet - at the new moon to call attention to its importance. But notice that he also instructs them to sound it again at the "time appointed." The Hebrew word translated as "time appointed" is *keseh* and is actually intended to mean "full moon." This is, as you know, two weeks after the appearance of the new moon. I believe this to mean that the shofar - the alarm - is to be sounded throughout the specific season God is alerting us to. Why? By sounding the shofar - which is believed to be a picture of the prophetic voice - at the time of the new moon and again at the full moon should be considered as representing the voice of two witnesses who are declaring the advent of a special season.

Scripture makes it clear that God always uses at least two witnesses to establish any truth.

"BY THE MOUTH OF TWO OR THREE WITNESSES THE MATTER SHALL BE ESTABLISHED." (DEUTERONOMY 19:15)

"I CALL HEAVEN AND EARTH AS WITNESSES TODAY AGAINST YOU, THAT I HAVE SET BEFORE YOU LIFE AND DEATH..." (DEUTERONOMY 30:19)

"But if he will not hear, take with you one or two more, that 'by the mouth of two or three witnesses every word may be established."
(Matthew 18:16)

"And I will give power to my two witnesses, and they will prophesy one thousand two hundred and sixty days, clothed in sackcloth."
(Revelation 11:3)

The greatest truth is that God sent His son as Messiah of the world and along with His Son, He sent the witnesses to establish this as truth. At His birth there were "wise men," meaning more than one (Mt. 2:1). When He was brought into the Temple for the first time, both Simeon and Anna acknowledged who He was (Luke 2). When John baptized Him, the appearance of a dove and the sound of the Father's voice identified Him as the Promised One (Mt. 3).

At His resurrection, two angels were in the tomb to announce that He was alive (Jn. 20:12). As He ascended, two men in white were there to pronounce that He would return again in like manner (Acts 1:10). Finally, in the last book of the Bible, both the Spirit and the Bride say, "come" (Rev. 22:17).

This hopefully demonstrates that any thing that is considered to be God-ordained is established by at least two witnesses. Consequently, that God has appointed times and that we should hearken unto these times and understand them is also established by at least two witnesses. The cycle of the moon - new moon and full moon - does this. The fact that the moon - one heavenly body - reflects the light of another luminary - the sun - further validates this.

THE PILGRIMAGE FEASTS

As I have already pointed out, the appropriate reason for sounding the shofar is to call us to attention. In the case of Psalm 81, we are being asked to notice and pay attention to the season we are entering into - a season that begins with the "new moon" and is highlighted by the "full moon." The fact that this season is regarded as a "solemn feast day" (in Hebrew *chag*), specifies this season as being during one of the seven "feasts of the Lord." Moreover, by using the moon and its cycle, Asaph actually pinpoints the **exact** season for us.

Of the seven Biblical feasts, only three are considered *chagim* or "solemn feast days." These are the three pilgrimage feasts during which Israel was to present themselves before the Lord. They are Unleavened Bread (Passover), Pentecost and Tabernacles. The Scripture declares:

"THREE TIMES A YEAR ALL YOUR MALES SHALL APPEAR BEFORE THE LORD YOUR GOD IN THE PLACE WHICH HE CHOOSES: AT THE FEAST OF UNLEAVENED BREAD, AT THE FEAST OF WEEKS, AND AT THE FEAST OF TABERNACLES; AND THEY SHALL NOT APPEAR BEFORE THE LORD EMPTY HANDED." (DEUTERONOMY 16:16)

The Feast of Unleavened Bread and the Feast of Weeks, more commonly known as Pentecost are feasts that fall in springtime. The Feast of Tabernacles comes later in the fall of the year. In fact, Tabernacles is the last of the seven feasts. Of the three mentioned, only two of them occur during a full moon - the Feast of Unleavened Bread and the Feast of Tabernacles. Of these two only the Feast of Tabernacles has a significant connection to the new moon - the other time Israel is instructed to blow the shofar.

Two weeks before the Feast of Tabernacles, on the new moon, there is another "appointed time" known in the Bible as *Yom Teruah*, but most commonly known as *Rosh Hashana*. This is the Feast of Trumpets when, of course, we are to "blow the shofar." In other words, the psalmist is calling attention to the "appointed times" that fall at the **end** of the biblical feast cycle. That we are to blow it at the "new moon" and "full moon" hints at the possibility that these two phases of the moon serve as witnesses of what God desires to do at this particular time of year.

Moreover, I will suggest to you that because this is the festival at the end of the cycle, perhaps there is something about them that is to be directed to those of God's people who are living "at the end." As a matter of fact, I find it extremely interesting that the new moon that begins the seventh Hebrew month called Tishri - a.k.a. *Rosh Hashana* - is also called *Chevlai shel Mashiach*, which means "birth pangs of the Messiah."

This is extremely interesting when you consider that *Rosh Hashana* is the only feast day that occurs on a new moon, meaning that *Rosh Hashana* can come without warning. Yes, there are signs that it is approaching, but like a woman in travail, no one knows exactly when that which is being birthed will appear. Hence, it is important to be in preparation for what is about to happen. One rabbinic adage puts it this way:

"THE MOON IS HIDING, KNOWING THAT THE DAY OF JUDGMENT IS COMING."

The Hebrew month in which these particular feast days occur - Rosh Hashana and Tabernacles - is called *Tishri*. On our calendar that would coincide with our September - October. (Because the Hebrew calendar is lunar, these feasts do not occur on the same day each year on our calendar.) This time of year and even the weeks leading up to it - beginning in August - are very important in God's prophetic cycles.

Because it is believed that this is the time of year for heavenly decisions, judgment and answered prayer, Jews are motivated to pursue God and renew their commitment to Him more than at any other time of year. In essence, they prepare for what is about to happen; something is about to be birthed. Thus, the weeks leading up to and including *Rosh Hashana* - Judgment Day - and the day when those judgments are sealed - *Yom Kippur* - is called *yamim teshuvah* or "days of repentance."

These "days of repentance" and the ramifications of this special season of God is the purpose of this teaching. The goal of this book is to thoroughly investigate the belief that just before the final feast days occur, God anticipates that His people will turn back to Him with their hearts, minds and otherwise. We must consider that it is during this time of national repentance that the "gates of heaven" are open even more than at other times of the year. We must also consider that if this season is God-ordained, then it bears significant ramifications, not just for Jews, but for Christians as well. In other words, how we as Christians view repentance can be enhanced, and in some cases corrected, when we understand the seasons of God.

Pastor Bob Rogers from Louisville, KY once related to me the story of how, after his father passed away, he saw him in a dream saying, "Bob. August is the month for answered prayer." Considering that August is typically the time when the days of repentance begin, it may be that this dream confirms everything we are about to teach you in this book. So, in order to more fully understand the "days of repentance," it is necessary to first have an accurate comprehension of God's view of seasons and cycles.

Chapter Two

UNDERSTANDING THE
IMPORTANCE OF CYCLES

"TO EVERYTHING THERE IS A SEASON, A TIME FOR EVERY PURPOSE UNDER HEAVEN: A TIME TO BE BORN, AND A TIME TO DIE; A TIME TO PLANT, AND A TIME TO PLUCK WHAT IS PLANTED; A TIME TO KILL, AND A TIME TO HEAL; A TIME TO BREAK DOWN, AND A TIME TO BUILD UP; A TIME TO WEEP, AND A TIME TO LAUGH; A TIME TO MOURN, AND A TIME TO DANCE; A TIME TO CAST AWAY STONES, AND A TIME TO GATHER STONES; A TIME TO EMBRACE, AND A TIME TO REFRAIN FROM EMBRACING; A TIME TO GAIN, AND A TIME TO LOSE; A TIME TO KEEP, AND A TIME TO THROW AWAY; A TIME TO TEAR, AND A TIME TO SEW; A TIME TO KEEP SILENCE, AND A TIME TO SPEAK; A TIME TO LOVE, AND A TIME TO HATE; A TIME OF WAR, AND A TIME OF PEACE." (ECCLESIASTES 3:1-8)

AN APPOINTED TIME

The Bible is full of passages that deal with time

and but more specifically, special seasons in time. For example, the Scripture mentions "seasons," "set times," "appointed times" and even the "fullness" of time" just to name a few.

"But My covenant I will establish with Isaac, whom Sarah shall bear to you at this **set time** next year." (Genesis 17:21)

"For Sarah conceived and bore Abraham a son in his old age, at the **set time** of which God had spoken to him." (Genesis 21:2)

"Then the LORD appointed a **set time**, saying, 'Tomorrow the LORD will do this thing in the land." (Exodus 9:5)

"Oh, that You would hide me in the grave, that You would conceal me until Your wrath is past, that You would appoint me a **set time,** and remember me!" (Job 14:13)

"And as it is **appointed** for men to die once, but after this the judgment." (Hebrews 9:27)

"And they will fall by the edge of the sword, and be led away captive into all nations. And Jerusalem will be trampled by Gentiles until **the times of the Gentiles** are fulfilled." (Luke 21:24)

"For I do not desire, brethren, that you

SHOULD BE IGNORANT OF THIS MYSTERY, LEST YOU SHOULD BE WISE IN YOUR OWN OPINION, THAT BLINDNESS IN PART HAS HAPPENED TO ISRAEL UNTIL **THE FULLNESS OF THE GENTILES** HAS COME IN." (ROMANS 11:25)

Even the coming of the Messiah was ordained to occur at a predetermined time.

"THAT IN THE DISPENSATION OF **THE FULLNESS OF THE TIMES** HE MIGHT GATHER TOGETHER IN ONE ALL THINGS IN CHRIST, BOTH WHICH ARE IN HEAVEN AND WHICH ARE ON EARTH IN HIM." (EPHESIANS 1:10)

"BUT WHEN THE **FULLNESS OF THE TIME** HAD COME, GOD SENT FORTH HIS SON, BORN OF A WOMAN, BORN UNDER THE LAW." (GALATIANS 4:4)

In each of these examples, when the time came, (or comes, whatever the case may be) for their fulfillment, that time is complete. At that point of completion, things begin to change. For instance, when the Hebrews had been in Egypt for the appointed four hundred years (Gen. 15:13), then came the Exodus. When Israel had been in Babylon for the appointed seventy years (Jer. 25:11), then came the return to Jerusalem.

What we learn from this is, when God sets an appointed time, it is a moment that He has personally marked for a display of His might and a demonstration of His faithfulness. He will perform His promises at the appointed time. Furthermore, if we look close enough at these examples, we can also discern a cyclical nature to these seasons and appointed times. In other words, things that have happened in the past teach us of things that will occur today and tomorrow. Solomon, the one who observed that there is a season for everything, said:

"THAT WHICH IS HAS ALREADY BEEN, AND WHAT IS TO BE HAS ALREADY BEEN; AND GOD REQUIRES AN ACCOUNT OF WHAT IS PAST." (ECCLESIASTES 3:15)

To put it another way; history is prophecy because everything occurs in cycles.

CYCLES OF NATURE

The origins of the word "cycle" is tied to the concept of something that moves in a circular motion repeatedly. Webster's defines a "cycle" as being, "any complete round or recurring series." It is also defined as, "a round of years or a recurring period of time, especially one in which certain events or phenomena repeat themselves in the same order and at the same intervals." We see this phenomena everywhere we look for Nature itself, created as the expression of the one and only God, is imbued with cycles.

Every twenty-four hours the earth completes its rotation thus giving us daylight in which to work and night time in which to sleep. Every 365.25 days, the earth completes its revolution around the sun marking a year. Within the period of a year, four very distinct seasons will make their presence known with certain signs - i.e. snow in Winter, flowers in Spring. And of course, we have the intricacies of the lunar cycle where every twenty-eight to thirty days, the moon completes its revolution around the earth marking a lunar month. We know when it begins by the "new moon." We know when it is half-way completed by the "full moon" and we know when it is concluding by the concealment of the moon.

Cycles are evident throughout nature. Even within the human race we see cycles. First comes birth, then infancy, then childhood followed by adolescence. Adolescence gives way to adulthood which eventually leads to old age and finally death - the circle of life. Adult women understand perfectly the efficiency and persistence of cycles. The point is, cycles and seasons are so much a part of our lives, that we tend to take it for granted and, as a consequence, sometimes overlook their importance.

If you doubt that to be true, then take a look at your wrist. More than likely there is something on it that you don't think about until you need it - your wristwatch. Now, take another look at the face of your watch and pay attention to what it is doing. It is marking time with hands that go round and round - in cyclical fashion!

When men have stopped to consider the importance of cycles, our desire to define them has at times proven difficult. One of the greatest challenges in marking these cycles and seasons was in fixing a consistent and accurate calendar. Thus, the primary timepiece for marking cycles has undergone many changes through the millennia.

The original Biblical calendar seems to have started out as a 360-day year. It was probably based on the cycle of the moon which is why, to this day, the Hebrew calendar is determined by the lunar cycle. However, history seems to indicate that it wasn't Hebrews alone who kept a 360-day calendar. The Greeks also had a calendar with twelve thirty-day months. The ancient Chinese and Indian cultures also determined a year to be 360 days. It is believed that what is known today as the Ka'aba in Mecca once housed 360 idols - one for each day of the year. Other ancient civilizations that used a 360-day calendar include the Romans, the Japanese, the Incas and the Mayans.

Eventually it proved necessary to adjust the calendar and so, in 46 BC, the Julian calendar was introduced by Julius Caesar and took effect in 45 BC. It was probably designed to approximate the tropical year, being a regular year of 365 days divided into 12 months, with a leap day added to February every four years. Hence the Julian year is on average 365.25 days long. However, there were inaccuracies in this calendar which led to established months and dates falling outside of their proper season. Over time this discrepancy accumulated significantly and forced a modification of the calendar.

The result was the Gregorian calendar, named so after Pope Gregory XIII, in 1582. This is the calendar that is currently used almost everywhere in the world. The point in all of this history is to show that, even though mankind sometimes overlooks the significance of seasons and cycles, we have nevertheless acknowledged their existence. That being said, most Christians never realize the significance of the most important seasons and cycles, and that is the seasons of God.

While the calendar is intended to help us mark time - to aid us in establishing when certain things are supposed to happen - the Bible, on the other hand, is intended to help us understand how God marks time. Consequently, His "calendar," if you will, is to alert us to when certain things important to His purposes are going to happen. It is with this in mind that I wish to discuss the importance of understanding more about Biblical cycles, and to elaborate on the special seasons ordained by God for His people alone.

HISTORY AND PROPHECY

"THE SONS OF ISSACHAR WHO HAD UNDERSTANDING OF THE TIMES, TO KNOW WHAT ISRAEL OUGHT TO DO, THEIR CHIEFS WERE TWO HUNDRED; AND ALL THEIR BRETHREN WERE AT THEIR COMMAND." (1 CHRONICLES 12:32)

The fact that everything is inherently cyclical is indication that God and His word are inherently cyclical as well. In other words, God establishes truth, works in the lives of men, and reveals this all to us according to times, seasons and cycles. For instance, through the prophet Hosea, God told Israel:

"When Israel was a child, I loved him, and out of Egypt I called My son." (Hosea 11:1)

This is first understood to be referring back to when Israel was in Egyptian bondage. When they cried out to the Lord, He sent a deliverer called Moses who was to tell Pharaoh:

"Thus says the LORD: 'Israel is My son, My firstborn.' " (Exodus 4:22)

And so, we understand that "My son" mentioned in Hosea 11:1 speaks of the nation of Israel. Yet, we also read where Joseph took Mary and the infant Messiah into Egypt to escape Herod the Great who was seeking to kill the child (Mt. 2:13-14). Matthew further records that Joseph's family remained in Egypt:

". . . until the death of Herod, that it might be fulfilled which was spoken by the Lord through the prophet, saying, 'Out of Egypt I called My Son.' "
(Matthew 2:15)

The prophecy Matthew alludes to is none other than Hosea 11:1. So if the Lord, speaking through the prophet, intended to recall to mind when He delivered His son Israel from Egyptian bondage, how is it that the verse in Hosea is also to be understood as being a Messianic prophecy? It is because, as I said before, history is prophecy. Knowing this to be true, the sons of Issachar were able to faithfully interpret the "times" so that Israel knew what to do.

The Hebrew word translated in 1 Chronicles 12 as "time" is *eth*. The root of this word means, "to set a firm hour." It is important to note that this word also conveys the idea that time is measured not only by the present, but by past occurrences and future expectations. So then, the meaning of this word is validating the concept that historical events are actually prophetic pictures. The primary Greek counterpart to this word is *chronos*. This Greek word is considered to be a "fixed space of time," for instance, from now until the coming of the LORD. If it is a "fixed time," why is it fixed? Perhaps, so that we can easily perceive its cyclical nature.

As an example of the cyclical nature of these "fixed times," consider the following oddity. Just prior to the destruction of the First Temple in Jerusalem, the Babylonians entered Israel thirty-three days after Passover. Centuries later, but still thirty-three days after Passover, the Romans entered Jerusalem, ultimately destroying the Second Temple. Apparently, because this "fixed time" repeated itself, God was trying to drive home a point to His people Israel. He used an fixed historical event - when the Babylonians entered Israel - to foreshadow another event that produced the same result - the Temple's destruction and the people's exile.

SPECIAL SEASONS OF GOD

"Seasons" are a particularly special event within a fixed time. The Greek word that denotes this type of occasion is *keiros*. This is understood to be a season when God visits the earth and His people. In Hebrew this most notable time of year is referred to as *moedim*, or "appointed times." We know that we can pray to the Father at any time and we also believe that His response is not limited to any special time table. However, we also understand that there are times and seasons that He considers "set apart" and it is these unique times that He desires a certain response from us. The *moedim* were when His people were to suspend their day-to-day routines and meet with the Lord.

If the President of the United States were to call and inform you that he had cleared his calendar on a particular day to meet especially with you, there is almost nothing that an average person wouldn't do in order to make the date. These special seasons, these *moedim*, are God's way of saying, "I have cleared my calendar to meet with you. Are you free?" If we would move heaven and earth to meet with the President, why should we be hesitant to meet with the sovereign of the Universe during these special times?

These seven *moedim* "appointed times" - the seven feasts of Israel - are notably featured on God's calendar and were fixed in accordance with cycles already inherent in nature - rain cycles and harvest cycles. In the spring and fall comes the rains - the former and the latter respectively. The harvest seasons -

so important to man's survival - are fixed as consequence of the rainy seasons. Thus, God appointed His times among these two important cycles because, ultimately, He desires to teach us that He alone is the One responsible for the rain that gives us the sustenance found at harvest.

But the lessons of the "appointed times" do not end there. In Israel's history, key events happened during these times of rain and harvest and, thus, God attached a significant historical event to an already existing season. This helped to ensure that His people would always remember His seasons and His cycles. And if that were not enough, these "appointed times" are also to teach of events that were yet to happen.

For instance, Joshua led Israel across the Jordan River and conquered Jericho during the time of Passover, Unleavened Bread and Firstfruits (Josh. 5:10-11). Solomon's Temple was dedicated during the time of the Feast of Tabernacles (2 Chr. 7). Nehemiah was restoring Jerusalem and the Temple during Tabernacles (Neh. 8).

Another dramatic example of how special seasons tend to be prophetic in nature is the 9th day of the Hebrew month *Av*. Though this day is not considered one of the seven *moedim*, it nevertheless seems to be a day that God Himself acknowledges as being special and fixed. Traditionally, it was on this day that the Babylonians destroyed the First Temple. Also, it is considered to be the day on which the Romans destroyed the Second Temple in 70 AD. Consequently, this day is acknowledged as being one of the worst in Israeli history.

It may be that these two events coincided with this day because, even before the destruction of the two Temples, another catastrophic event had occurred. It is believed that centuries before there was a temple, ten of the twelve spies sent by Moses to tour the land returned with an evil report on 9 Av. On that same day, God condemned all but Joshua and Caleb to die in the wilderness. Maybe this is what set the tone, or shall I say, "fixed the time" for other future devastating incidents in Israeli history. It certainly seems that, as if to concur with their view of this day, God indeed allowed other tragic events to occur on this day throughout history. Consider what has happened on 9 Av since 70 AD.

❖ Bar Kochba Rebellion defeated. (135 A.D.)
❖ Jews expelled from England. (1290 AD)
❖ Expulsion of Jews from Spain commences. (1492 AD).
❖ 3,000 Jews murdered in Russia. (1648 AD)
❖ Jews expelled from Austria. (1670 AD)
❖ Turkey bars the immigration of Jews into Palestine (1882 AD)
❖ World War I began (1914).

The same "phenomena" can be observed when we take other significant dates or fixed times in Israeli past and look at them throughout history. In fact, there are literally hundreds of examples of this nature. Notwithstanding, the most valuable lesson and the most poignant feature found in God's special seasons and, specifically His *moedim*, is the Messiah. Speaking of Christ, the Scripture declares that:

"THEN I SAID, 'BEHOLD, I COME; IN THE SCROLL OF THE BOOK IT IS WRITTEN OF ME.' " (PSALM 40:7)

THE SEVEN MOEDIM

All of God's appointed times are "fixed' during certain seasons and will always occur at the same time year after year on the Hebrew calendar. So, let us briefly examine the importance of each of these feasts on God's calendar. Before doing so, I should point out that, like other calendars, the Hebrew calendar has undergone some changes.

Today's Hebrew calendar is approximately 354 days based on the lunar cycle. Yet, it also brings the positioning of the earth in relation to the sun into the equation as well. The way it does this is by adding an extra month - 2 Adar - eleven times during a seventeen year cycle. In essence, the modern Hebrew calendar is technically a luna-solar calendar (i.e. based on the moon *and* the sun). Not only that, but the Hebrew calendar is actually viewed as being two calendars in one - a civil and religious calendar.

The distinction is made between the two, in part, due to the fact that, early in the world's history, the first month of the year was what is now known as *Tishri*. To be more specific, this was the beginning of the year up until the time of the Exodus. But with the Exodus God made a change in the calendar and that change gave birth to what is regarded as the religious calendar. More importantly, this change helps us to see how God views time and seasons.

"Now the LORD spoke to Moses and Aaron in the land of Egypt, saying, 'This month shall be your beginning of months; it shall be the first month of the year to you.' " (Exodus 12:1-2)

The month referred to as "this month" is called *Nisan* on modern Hebrew calendars but its more appropriate biblical name is *Aviv*. The month of *Aviv* comes in the spring time of the year. In fact, *aviv* means "springtime" because it is associated with the time when green ears of barley begin to appear, demonstrating that life is re-emerging after the long dead winter. This is why it is the month that initiates the spiritual or religious calendar. It should then come as no surprise that it is during this month - when life returns to that which was dead - that God ordained an appointed time that would prove to be the most important in the lives of all those who would believe.

"On the fourteenth day of the first month at twilight is the LORD's Passover." (Leviticus 23:5)

Pesach or Passover, the first of the seven *moedim* as well as the first of the three pilgrimage feasts - the feasts where Israeli males were commanded to appear for the Lord - commemorates the Exodus from Egyptian slavery wrought by the blood of a lamb. The Passover, prepared on the fourteenth day of the first month, *Aviv*, marks the deliverance from oppression and the salvation of God's people. Most importantly, the Passover speaks of the Lamb of God who takes away the sins of the world and His crucifixion.

When Israel sat down to eat the Passover, they would also partake of *matzah* or unleavened bread. Passover actually initiates the Feast of Unleavened Bread (*Hag ha Matzot*), an appointed time which lasts for the next seven days.

"AND ON THE FIFTEENTH DAY OF THE SAME MONTH IS THE FEAST OF UNLEAVENED BREAD TO THE LORD; SEVEN DAYS YOU MUST EAT UNLEAVENED BREAD." (LEVITICUS 23:6)

This week of abstaining from leaven is intended to teach us of the importance of removing sin from our homes. By purging our dwellings of leaven, we learn to discipline ourselves and expunge destructive habits from our lives.

"THEREFORE PURGE OUT THE OLD LEAVEN, THAT YOU MAY BE A NEW LUMP, SINCE YOU TRULY ARE UNLEAVENED. FOR INDEED CHRIST, OUR PASSOVER, WAS SACRIFICED FOR US." (1 CORINTHIANS 5:7)

The Feast of Unleavened Bread also serves to remind us that the One who "was made sin" was placed in a tomb before rising from the dead to become the "first fruits."

On the first day of the week, after the seven days of Unleavened Bread had begun, worshippers in Jerusalem would bring the first fruits of their barley harvest, the first of the year, to Jerusalem. This was in celebration of the Feast of First Fruits. Celebrants would ascend the steps of the Temple and bring a sheaf to wave before the Lord in accordance with His commandment.

"Speak to the children of Israel, and say to them: When you come into the land which I give to you, and reap its harvest, then you shall bring a sheaf of the firstfruits of your harvest to the priest. He shall wave the sheaf before the Lord, to be accepted on your behalf; on the day after the Sabbath the priest shall wave it." (Leviticus 23:10-11)

On the first day of the week following the crucifixion of Jesus, Jews would have been ascending the steps of the Temple to bring the first fruits of their harvest in celebration First Fruits. On that very same day, we know that Jesus rose from the dead. Scripture tells us that when the Messiah rose from the dead and became the "first fruits" of many brethren, those saints who had fallen asleep were raised with him. These He presented unto the Father.

"The graves were opened; and many bodies of the saints who had fallen asleep were raised; and

COMING OUT OF THE GRAVES AFTER HIS RESURRECTION, THEY WENT INTO THE HOLY CITY AND APPEARED TO MANY." (MATTHEW 27:52-53)

"WHEN HE ASCENDED ON HIGH, HE LED CAPTIVITY CAPTIVE, AND GAVE GIFTS TO MEN." (EPHESIANS 4:8)

"BUT NOW CHRIST IS RISEN FROM THE DEAD, AND HAS BECOME THE FIRSTFRUITS OF THOSE WHO HAVE FALLEN ASLEEP." (1 CORINTHIANS 15:20)

In these first three spring festivals, we see how the "appointed times" were fixed so that God's Plan would be made known. Not only that but, for centuries prior to these events, Israel would actually have been rehearsing for the coming of the Messiah - His death, burial and resurrection - albeit unwittingly.

These first three festivals prepare God's people for the next very important pilgrimage festival called Pentecost.

"AND YOU SHALL COUNT FOR YOURSELVES FROM THE DAY AFTER THE SABBATH, FROM THE DAY THAT YOU BROUGHT THE SHEAF OF THE WAVE OFFERING: SEVEN SABBATHS SHALL BE COMPLETED. COUNT FIFTY DAYS TO THE DAY AFTER THE SEVENTH SABBATH; THEN YOU SHALL OFFER A NEW GRAIN OFFERING TO THE LORD. YOU SHALL BRING FROM YOUR DWELLINGS TWO WAVE LOAVES OF TWO TENTHS OF AN EPHAH. THEY SHALL BE OF FINE FLOUR; THEY SHALL BE BAKED WITH LEAVEN. THEY ARE THE FIRST FRUITS TO THE LORD." (LEVITICUS 23:15-17)

Pentecost (which means "fiftieth") is called in Hebrew, *Shavuot*, or the "Feast of Weeks." It is regarded as such because it comes seven weeks after or on the fiftieth day following the Feast of First Fruits. The first observance of *Shavuot* occurred when Israel was given the Torah at Mt. Sinai, and thus, the "church in the wilderness" was born (see Ex. 19 & 20). Fifteen hundred years after that historical event, Christ's disciples experienced a similar revelation that gave birth to the Church of Jesus Christ (see Acts 2). Again, we see why it was important to observe God's appointed times - so that the fulfillment of these appointed times would be more readily acknowledged.

After Pentecost comes an interval of several months until the next appointed time. Then in early Autumn comes the first of the three fall festivals, *Yom Teruah*, also known as *Rosh Hashana* ("head of the year") or the Feast of Trumpets.

"SPEAK TO THE CHILDREN OF ISRAEL, SAYING: IN THE SEVENTH MONTH, ON THE FIRST DAY OF THE MONTH, YOU SHALL HAVE A SABBATH REST, A MEMORIAL OF BLOWING OF TRUMPETS, A HOLY CONVOCATION." (LEVITICUS 23:24)

This feast day, falling on the first day of the seventh month, *Tishri*, is noted for being the day on which trumpets are blown. The biblical trumpet, the *shofar* or ram's horn, is an important component of this appointed time. The *Mishnah*, in fact, places an incredible degree of importance on the shofar. According to this rabbinic work, it is used to announce the beginning of festivals, to muster troops, to warn of danger, to assemble the people and for coronations.

Because it is believed that Adam was created on the day that would later become the Feast of Trumpets and because the creation of mankind was considered to be the crowning achievement of God's handiwork, the anniversary of this event has become the day associated with the coronation of the King of the Universe. Of course, this will be ultimately personified in the Messiah, who is the "resurrection and the life" (Jn. 11:25). Consequently, the Feasts of Trumpets ties the coronation of the King to the future resurrection of the dead.

"IN A MOMENT, IN THE TWINKLING OF AN EYE, AT THE LAST TRUMPET. FOR THE TRUMPET WILL SOUND, AND THE DEAD WILL BE RAISED INCORRUPTIBLE, AND WE SHALL BE CHANGED. FOR THIS CORRUPTIBLE MUST PUT ON INCORRUPTION, AND THIS MORTAL MUST PUT ON IMMORTALITY."

(1 CORINTHIANS 15:52-53)

Through the writings of Paul, we see that the trumpet or *shofar* is a significant component of the future resurrection. In fact, this is one of the ten reasons for the blowing of the shofar as related by Rabbi Se'adiah Gaon. Some of the other purposes he assigns to the sounding of the shofar are:

❖ The creation of mankind.

❖ The binding of Isaac.
❖ To remind us of the words of the prophets.
❖ The first day of the Ten days of Repentance.
❖ To anticipate the ingathering of the dispersed of Israel.
❖ To recall the coming day of Judgment.

The coming Judgment Day referred to is, in fact, regarded as *Yom Teruah* or the Feast of Trumpets. Because it is Judgment Day, it is important to anticipate this before hand and thus the season leading up to *Yom Teruah* is a time of *teshuvah* or "repentance." The shofar is blown then to alert us to the approaching Day of Judgment. But the sound of the shofar does not end on *Yom Teruah*, but on *Yom Kippur*. It is said in Judaism that, "All things are judged on Rosh Hashana but Fate is sealed on Yom Kippur."

So, we understand that the most dramatic of the feasts is *Yom Kippur* or the Day of Atonement. This "appointed time" falls on the tenth day of the month *Tishri*. This is the day when the High Priest entered the Most Holy Place to sprinkle blood upon the Ark of the Covenant and to intermediate for the sins of national Israel. During this time, no one spoke until after the High Priest had consummated his solemn duties. When he had finished his task, all Israel trusted that the merciful God had accepted their acts of repentance.

"ALSO THE TENTH DAY OF THIS SEVENTH MONTH

SHALL BE THE DAY OF ATONEMENT. IT SHALL BE A HOLY CON-
VOCATION FOR YOU; YOU SHALL AFFLICT YOUR SOULS, AND
OFFER AN OFFERING MADE BY FIRE TO THE LORD. AND YOU
SHALL DO NO WORK ON THAT SAME DAY, FOR IT IS THE DAY
OF ATONEMENT, TO MAKE ATONEMENT FOR YOU BEFORE THE
LORD YOUR GOD." (LEVITICUS 23:27-28)

We understand that Christ, our High Priest, has
become our advocate before God and has atoned for
our sins once and for all time when He offered His
own blood on our behalf. The writer of Hebrews
records that:

"NOT WITH THE BLOOD OF GOATS AND CALVES, BUT
WITH HIS OWN BLOOD HE ENTERED THE MOST HOLY PLACE
ONCE FOR ALL, HAVING OBTAINED ETERNAL REDEMPTION.
FOR IF THE BLOOD OF BULLS AND GOATS AND THE ASHES OF
A HEIFER, SPRINKLING THE UNCLEAN, SANCTIFIES FOR THE
PURIFYING OF THE FLESH, HOW MUCH MORE SHALL THE
BLOOD OF CHRIST, WHO THROUGH THE ETERNAL SPIRIT
OFFERED HIMSELF WITHOUT SPOT TO GOD, CLEANSE YOUR
CONSCIENCE FROM DEAD WORKS TO SERVE THE LIVING
GOD?" (HEBREWS 9:12-14)

Even though we see how Jesus has fulfilled
this feast, because all things of God are cyclical in
nature, I believe that we will see a future fulfillment of
this unique day as well. During the future Tribulation,
the Scripture says that the Heavenly High Priest will
enter into the Most Holy Place in Heaven.

"WHEN HE OPENED THE SEVENTH SEAL, THERE WAS SILENCE IN HEAVEN FOR ABOUT HALF AN HOUR. AND I SAW THE SEVEN ANGELS WHO STAND BEFORE GOD, AND TO THEM WERE GIVEN SEVEN TRUMPETS. THEN ANOTHER ANGEL, HAVING A GOLDEN CENSER, CAME AND STOOD AT THE ALTAR. HE WAS GIVEN MUCH INCENSE, THAT HE SHOULD OFFER IT WITH THE PRAYERS OF ALL THE SAINTS UPON THE GOLDEN ALTAR WHICH WAS BEFORE THE THRONE. AND THE SMOKE OF THE INCENSE, WITH THE PRAYERS OF THE SAINTS, ASCENDED BEFORE GOD FROM THE ANGEL'S HAND. THEN THE ANGEL TOOK THE CENSER, FILLED IT WITH FIRE FROM THE ALTAR, AND THREW IT TO THE EARTH. AND THERE WERE NOISES, THUNDERINGS, LIGHTNINGS, AND AN EARTHQUAKE."

(REVELATION 8:1-5)

The last of the festivals (and also the last of the three pilgrimage festivals) is the feast called *Sukkot* or the Feast of Tabernacles.

"SPEAK TO THE CHILDREN OF ISRAEL, SAYING, THE FIFTEENTH DAY OF THIS SEVENTH MONTH SHALL BE THE FEAST OF TABERNACLES FOR SEVEN DAYS TO THE LORD."

(LEVITICUS 23:34)

This is the festival where Israel commemorates the forty years of wandering through the wilderness. During this time they had no permanent residence and so, they dwelt in temporary booths or *sukkot*. To offset this inconvenience, they could claim the distinction of being the only people in the world who enjoyed the presence of the one and only God. It was in the

Camp of Israel that the Lord Himself tabernacled. This is why we understand Tabernacles to speak ultimately of the coming Millennial Kingdom of Christ when He will dwell - tabernacle - in our midst.

In fact, it is important to note that *all* of these feasts will be observed during the Reign of Messiah. The Marriage Supper of the Lamb (Rev. 19:7, 9) is most likely going to be a Passover Seder. The Passover is the only meal mentioned in the Bible whose focus is a lamb. Furthermore, remember that Jesus told His disciples that He would not eat the Passover *until* He could share it with His disciples in the Kingdom.

"THEN HE SAID TO THEM, 'WITH FERVENT DESIRE I HAVE DESIRED TO EAT THIS PASSOVER WITH YOU BEFORE I SUFFER; FOR I SAY TO YOU, I WILL NO LONGER EAT OF IT UNTIL IT IS FULFILLED IN THE KINGDOM OF GOD.' THEN HE TOOK THE CUP, AND GAVE THANKS, AND SAID, 'TAKE THIS AND DIVIDE IT AMONG YOURSELVES; FOR I SAY TO YOU, I WILL NOT DRINK OF THE FRUIT OF THE VINE UNTIL THE KINGDOM OF GOD COMES.' " (LUKE 22:15-18)

The Bible makes it clear that all nations will be required to keep the Feast of Tabernacles.

"AND IT SHALL COME TO PASS THAT EVERYONE WHO IS LEFT OF ALL THE NATIONS WHICH CAME AGAINST JERUSALEM SHALL GO UP FROM YEAR TO YEAR TO WORSHIP THE KING, THE LORD OF HOSTS, AND TO KEEP THE FEAST OF TABERNACLES. AND IT SHALL BE THAT WHICHEVER OF THE

FAMILIES OF THE EARTH DO NOT COME UP TO JERUSALEM TO WORSHIP THE KING, THE LORD OF HOSTS, ON THEM THERE WILL BE NO RAIN. IF THE FAMILY OF EGYPT WILL NOT COME UP AND ENTER IN, THEY SHALL HAVE NO RAIN; THEY SHALL RECEIVE THE PLAGUE WITH WHICH THE LORD STRIKES THE NATIONS WHO DO NOT COME UP TO KEEP THE FEAST OF TABERNACLES. THIS SHALL BE THE PUNISHMENT OF EGYPT AND THE PUNISHMENT OF ALL THE NATIONS THAT DO NOT COME UP TO KEEP THE FEAST OF TABERNACLES."

(ZECHARIAH 14:16-19)

Notice also how Ezekiel describes the worship that occurs at the Temple during the Millennial Reign.

"THUS SAYS THE LORD GOD: THE GATEWAY OF THE INNER COURT THAT FACES TOWARD THE EAST SHALL BE SHUT THE SIX WORKING DAYS; BUT ON THE SABBATH IT SHALL BE OPENED, AND ON THE DAY OF THE NEW MOON IT SHALL BE OPENED. THE PRINCE SHALL ENTER BY WAY OF THE VESTIBULE OF THE GATEWAY FROM THE OUTSIDE, AND STAND BY THE GATEPOST. THE PRIESTS SHALL PREPARE HIS BURNT OFFERING AND HIS PEACE OFFERINGS. HE SHALL WORSHIP AT THE THRESHOLD OF THE GATE. THEN HE SHALL GO OUT, BUT THE GATE SHALL NOT BE SHUT UNTIL EVENING. LIKEWISE THE PEOPLE OF THE LAND SHALL WORSHIP AT THE ENTRANCE TO THIS GATEWAY BEFORE THE LORD ON THE SABBATHS AND THE NEW MOONS. THE BURNT OFFERING THAT THE PRINCE OFFERS TO THE LORD ON THE SABBATH DAY SHALL BE SIX LAMBS WITHOUT BLEMISH, AND A RAM WITHOUT BLEMISH; AND THE GRAIN OFFERING SHALL BE ONE EPHAH FOR A RAM, AND THE GRAIN OFFERING FOR THE LAMBS, AS MUCH AS

HE WANTS TO GIVE, AS WELL AS A HIN OF OIL WITH EVERY EPHAH. ON THE DAY OF THE NEW MOON IT SHALL BE A YOUNG BULL WITHOUT BLEMISH, SIX LAMBS, AND A RAM; THEY SHALL BE WITHOUT BLEMISH." (EZEKIEL 46:1-6)

The point is that God's methodology has not and will not change. These "appointed times" were fixed at the beginning and for all time. Therefore, they will be observed and celebrated during the Millennium just as they were celebrated centuries ago. Therefore, I suggest that if they were relevant in the past and will be relevant in the future, they are also relevant presently! Should we not pay heed to God's appointed times and seasons and learn the lessons they teach us and especially since they teach us of the Messiah and all that God intends for His people?

RIVERS OF LIVING WATER

All aspects of these appointed times are unique in celebration and meaning. Even the sacrifices and offerings brought to each of these festivals speak of something spiritually significant. For instance, during the Passover season, besides offering a lamb, celebrants would bring the first fruits of their barley harvest and offer it to God, prophesying of the first fruits of the dead to be presented to the Father through the resurrection of the Messiah.

At Pentecost they would bring the firstfruits of their wheat harvest. During this observance, two loaves of leavened bread - as opposed to the unleavened bread at Passover - were baked and waved before the Lord. This was to signify that there would be two different groups of people - Jews and Gentile - who were to comprise the whole house of Israel. That these two groups were "leavened" or of a sinful nature and could nevertheless be presented to God was possible only because of the One who was made sin for us - the unleavened bread of Passover - and who died in order to bring forth much fruit (Jn. 12:24).

On the last day of the Feast of Tabernacles, water is poured out upon the altar in a ceremony known as the water libation. This would begin when a large group of people would follow the priest from the Temple to the spring called, in Hebrew, *Shiloah*. We know it as the pool of Siloam. The priest carried a golden vessel with which he would draw water from this spring. The water, regarded as *mayim chayim* or "living water" was to be poured upon the altar.

When the priest arrived at the spring, a shofar was sounded to alert the people. Using his golden vessel, the priest withdrew the water while reciting the prophet Isaiah who wrote:

"THEREFORE WITH JOY YOU WILL DRAW WATER FROM THE WELLS OF SALVATION." (ISAIAH 12:3)

As he prepared to return to the Temple, a group of priests took large willow branches and formed two lines on either side of the priest carrying the "living water." Together, they continued on in this procession and as they did, the priests carrying the willow branches waved them to and fro creating a "wind" effect. At the same time, a flute was piped by another priest referred to as "the pierced one." He was symbolically calling for the wind and water to enter the Temple.

The procession would end at the altar where sacrifices were made. At this point, the golden vessel containing the "living water" and another silver vessel containing wine were both emptied into a common spout causing the two to mix. This mixture of water and wine was thus poured out onto the altar. Those who carried the willow branches marched around the altar seven times and then covered the altar with their branches.

This was a time of such great celebration and joy that one rabbinic writing declared

"HE WHO NEVER SAW THE REJOICING OF THE DRAWING OF THE WATER NEVER SAW REJOICING IN HIS LIFE."

It was during all of this celebration that Jesus stood up and announced that He was that well of salvation, the well of living water.

"ON THE LAST DAY, THAT GREAT DAY OF THE FEAST, JESUS STOOD AND CRIED OUT, SAYING, 'IF ANYONE THIRSTS, LET HIM COME TO ME AND DRINK. HE WHO BELIEVES IN ME, AS THE SCRIPTURE HAS SAID, OUT OF HIS HEART WILL FLOW RIVERS OF LIVING WATER.' BUT THIS HE SPOKE CONCERNING THE SPIRIT, WHOM THOSE BELIEVING IN HIM WOULD RECEIVE, FOR THE HOLY SPIRIT WAS NOT YET GIVEN, BECAUSE JESUS WAS NOT YET GLORIFIED." (JOHN 7:37-39)

Jesus was and is most literally the source of living water. In fact, the Hebrew word translated in Isaiah 12:3 as "salvation" is *yeshua*. Yeshua, as many of you know, is the Hebrew name from which we get "Jesus." At His death, witnesses noticed that both blood and water issued from His side reminding us of the wine and water that were "poured out" upon the altar of God. And of course His death gave birth to the outpouring of the Holy Spirit, the *ruach* or "wind."

And so we see that even the offerings of God's appointed time contain many lessons and yet, many Christians remain ignorant of God's special seasons.

OTHER IMPORTANT SEASONS

Perhaps you noticed earlier that when Ezekiel described the worship in the Millennial Temple, he mentioned other special days that God has designated as appointed times. These other holy days have been observed by Jews just as faithfully as the seven *moedim*. The most prominent of these other holy days is the weekly Sabbath. Every seventh day is considered to be a *Yom Tov* (literally, "good day" or holy day). Consequently the weekly sabbath, along with the other sabbaths, is considered to be an "appointed time."

Other holy days include *Rosh Chodesh* ("head of the month"), or the New Moon. Every seventh year is regarded as the *shemmitah* year, or a sabbatical for the land. Every fiftieth year is the *yovel*, or Jubilee. Like the seven Feasts of the Lord, these holy days also teach us important lessons about the covenant and our relationship with God. Through all of these appointed times, God teaches us about Himself, His methods and His purposes. In short, if one doesn't understand cycles, and more importantly God's appointed times and cycles, it is going to be very difficult to understand how to properly interact with God.

There are still other holidays celebrated during the course of the year that are not necessarily considered to be *moedim*, "appointed times." They are mainly festivals that were commissioned as the result of an historical, and might I say, miraculous event. For instance, *Purim* (the Feast of "lots") is celebrated because of the miraculous delivery of the Jewish people during the time of Esther. Likewise, *Hanukkah* (the Feast of Dedication) commemorates the time when the Jewish people were delivered from the Syrian despot Antiochus Epiphanes and were able to rededicate the temple and rekindle the Holy Menorah.

Even though God did not officially ordain these celebrations, He nevertheless was responsible for the deliverance of His people during these times. Also, throughout the history of Israel, significant events have occurred during Purim and Hanukkah demonstrating God's acknowledgment of and participation in these special seasons.

For instance, when during the first Gulf War Saddam Hussein was pelting Israel with Scud missiles, many Israelis were fearful of death by gas or even worse. Even though Saddam's main threat was from the U.S., he determined to focus his worst threat against Israel. He finally had to concede that he was defeated and so, in February 1991, he relented, gave in to the US-led coalition's demands and requested a cease fire. That cease fire came on Purim.

This example is meant to demonstrate that God determines certain things to happen during certain times of the year - at these appointed times. Let me make this clear - the Bible is to be understood as being a book about cycles and seasons and, more importantly, what God wishes to manifest during these seasons.

Chapter Three

THE SEASON OF REPENTANCE

"IN THOSE DAYS JOHN THE BAPTIST CAME PREACHING IN THE WILDERNESS OF JUDEA, AND SAYING, 'REPENT, FOR THE KINGDOM OF HEAVEN IS AT HAND!' " (MATTHEW 3:1-2)

In the previous chapter, we established biblically that God ordained certain seasons and cycles during which He would cause singular events to occur. Throughout the Bible, we see Him manifesting Himself in different ways at different times. In John's Gospel we read that an angel would visit the Pool of Bethesda at a certain "season to trouble the water" (Jn. 5:4). The Scripture tells us that in due season we shall reap "if we faint not" (Gal. 6:9) and to be instant "in season and out of season" (2 Tim. 4:2). Miraculous things do occur during these special times and seasons.

Before John the Baptist was born, we learn that his father, Zechariah, was told of his impending birth, of his life's purpose and that "the words would be fulfilled in their season" (Lk. 1:20). The "words" he referred to were the words that defined John's mission. The Scripture says of John that:

"HE WILL **TURN** MANY OF THE CHILDREN OF ISRAEL TO THE LORD THEIR GOD. HE WILL ALSO GO BEFORE HIM IN THE SPIRIT AND POWER OF ELIJAH, TO **TURN** THE HEARTS OF THE FATHERS TO THE CHILDREN, AND THE DISOBEDIENT TO THE WISDOM OF THE JUST, TO MAKE READY A PEOPLE PREPARED FOR THE LORD." (LUKE 1:16-17)

And thus, we understand that John was considered to be equivalent to the prophet Elijah in purpose and in destiny. This truth is validated by the Messiah Himself when He said:

"FOR ALL THE PROPHETS AND THE LAW PROPHESIED UNTIL JOHN. AND IF YOU ARE WILLING TO RECEIVE IT, HE IS ELIJAH WHO IS TO COME. HE WHO HAS EARS TO HEAR, LET HIM HEAR!" (MATTHEW 11:13-15)

On another occasion, Matthew records that:

"JESUS ANSWERED AND SAID TO THEM, 'INDEED, ELIJAH IS COMING FIRST AND WILL RESTORE ALL THINGS. BUT I SAY TO YOU THAT ELIJAH HAS COME ALREADY, AND THEY DID NOT KNOW HIM BUT DID TO HIM WHATEVER THEY WISHED'. . . THEN THE DISCIPLES UNDERSTOOD THAT HE SPOKE TO THEM OF JOHN THE BAPTIST."
(MATTHEW 17:11-13)

So, in order to fully understood John's mission

as the forerunner to the Messiah, it becomes necessary to understand Elijah's purpose and ministry and specifically his end-time ministry. Through the prophet Malachi, the Lord ordained that before the coming day of the Lord, He would send Elijah the prophet (Mal. 4:5) but for what purpose? According to the prophecy, Elijah comes to accomplish something specific.

"BEHOLD, I WILL SEND YOU ELIJAH THE PROPHET BEFORE THE COMING OF THE GREAT AND DREADFUL DAY OF THE LORD. AND HE WILL **TURN** THE HEARTS OF THE FATHERS TO THE CHILDREN, AND THE HEARTS OF THE CHILDREN TO THEIR FATHERS, LEST I COME AND STRIKE THE EARTH WITH A CURSE." (MALACHI 4:5-6)

To turn the hearts of the fathers to the children and the hearts of the children to the fathers is exactly what the angel announced John was being sent to do (Lk. 1:17). He was to come and provoke the people - the children - to "turn." In Hebrew, "turn" comes from the root *shuv*. This word literally means "to turn back" - to turn back into the direction from which you came. Perhaps a better way to put it would be to "return." The implication of course is to "return" to the Lord.

This word *shuv* is the root word from which we obtain the word *teshuvah*, translated in English as "repentance." In short, Elijah's end-time mission is to call God's people to repentance - to return to Him - before that great and dreadful day. Consequently, this was also John's mission as forerunner to the Messiah.

So when John arrived on the scene, we shouldn't be surprised to see that he came calling the people to return to the Lord. Why? Because the Kingdom of Heaven was "at hand" meaning that the "day of the Lord" was approaching. He came preaching repentance - *teshuvah* - and specifically during a **season** that preceded the advent of a great and ominous event - the arrival of the Lord. Therefore, we are to understand that all great and miraculous events in the lives of God's people are always initiated by *teshuvah* - repentance.

[handwritten margin note: today the awaited event is the second coming]

DAYS OF REPENTANCE

From a Hebraic perspective, it has always been understood that the holy festival called *Yom Kippur* or "Day of Atonement" was symbolic of the coming "day of the Lord." The reason for this association is the ominous tone of the day. It was on this day that the High Priest would enter into the Most Holy Place, into the very Presence of the Most High God, to make atonement for himself and for all the congregation of Israel. Their fortune, not to mention their very lives, depended on the outcome of this day. So, when it became apparent that God had forgiven their sins - by virtue of the scarlet thread that miraculously turned white (Isa. 1:18) - then Israel was prepared to enter the next prominent and most joyous of all seasons, the Feast of Tabernacles.

Sukkot or the Feast of Tabernacles is the particular feast that has always been synonymous with the Kingdom. So, when John announced that the "Kingdom of Heaven was at hand," he was, in effect, alluding to a season on God's timetable hinted at by the feast called *Sukkot*. That he also admonished the people to first repent, speaks of the approaching Day of the Lord - a season hinted at by *Yom Kippur*. However, it is must be understood that the all-important repentance must take place **before** the great and dreadful day of the Lord and **before** the Kingdom. In other words, *teshuvah* must begin before these appointed times. Consequently, there is an appointed time for *teshuvah* itself.

As I noted earlier, the fall feasts which include *Yom Kippur* and *Sukkot* actually begin with *Yom Teruah* (a.k.a *Rosh Hashana*) or the Feast of Trumpets. This, the first day of the month *Tishri*, is an extremely important day in biblical history. On this day:

- ❖ The Tabernacle was set up (Ex. 40:2)
- ❖ The Temple was sanctified (2 Chr. 29:17)
- ❖ The Jews returned from captivity (Ezra 7:9)
- ❖ The priests separated from strange wives (Ezra 10:17)

Recall that this feast day is also referred to as *Yom ha Din* - the future Day of Judgment. If this is the day when God judges man then it would behoove us to repent **before** the Day of Judgment and the subsequent feast days - *Yom Kippur* and *Sukkot*.

Understanding this fully, Judaism has long acknowledged that the Hebrew month of *Elul* is the beginning of the season of *teshuvah*.

Because it is the Hebrew month that precedes the month of *Tishri*, *Elul* begins thirty days before the Feast of Trumpets. Beginning on the first day of *Elul* and continuing throughout the entire month, the shofar or ram's horn is blown to indicate that the season of *teshuvah* or "repentance" has begun. And so, God's people set their hearts to "turn back" to God, to His Word and to His ways. By announcing the advent of the season of repentance, the shofar really serves to remind God's people of the approach of Judgment Day. Thus, the alarming sound of the shofar - symbolically the voice of God - is to awaken those who are slumbering to the need to hastily return to the Holy One of Israel.

Indeed, the Apostle Paul echoed this warning when he admonished God's people to awake so that we might return to God. He said:

"Now it is high time to awake out of sleep; for now our salvation is nearer than when we first believed. The night is far spent, the day is at hand. Therefore let us cast off the works of darkness, and let us put on the armor of light. Let us walk properly, as in the day, not in revelry and drunkenness, not in lewdness and lust, not in strife and envy." (Romans 13:11-13)

"Awake, you who sleep. Arise from the dead,

AND CHRIST WILL GIVE YOU LIGHT. SEE THEN THAT YOU WALK CIRCUMSPECTLY, NOT AS FOOLS BUT AS WISE, REDEEMING THE TIME, BECAUSE THE DAYS ARE EVIL."

(EPHESIANS 5:14-16)

Due to the seriousness of our need to repent, and so that we will not forget to turn to God with all our hearts, the shofar is repeatedly blown for the entire thirty-day period of the month *Elul*. And so, the thirty days of *Elul* are considered to be a time to reflect upon your destiny; a time to seek God concerning your spiritual future and a time to obtain mercy. With this particular thought in mind, it is interesting to note that the Hebrew spelling of *Elul* forms an acronym for the Hebrew phrase *ani l'dodi v'dodi li* - "I am my beloved's and my beloved is mine" (Song 6:3).

אלול

Elul

אני לדודי ודודי לי

ani l'dodi v'dodi li

It is most important to remember that, above all, the month of *Elul* is a time to prepare for judgment. The thirty-first day of this season of repentance is *Yom Teruah* - the first day of the month *Tishri*. On this day, the shofar is sounded repeatedly throughout the day for this is, in fact, the Feast of Trumpets. The shofar will continue to be sounded right up until the Day of Atonement which falls on the tenth day of the month of *Tishri*. Therefore, from 1 *Elul* through 10 *Tishri* accounts for a total of forty days of *teshuvah* - repentance.

This is a long-held tradition in Judaism, so long in fact, that its origins seem to go all the way back to Mt. Sinai. The Encyclopedia Judaica states that the tradition:

". . . CONNECTS THE FORTY DAYS (OF TESHUVAH) WITH MOSES STAYING ON MT. SINAI FORTY DAYS (EX. 34:28), WHICH WAS CALCULATED TO HAVE COMMENCED ON THE FIRST OF ELUL AND ENDED ON THE 10TH OF TISHRI (THE DAY OF ATONEMENT)." - VOLUME 6, PAGE 690

And so for clarity, here is a summary of the forty days of *Teshuvah*.

❖ Elul 1 - Elul 30 (first thirty days of *Teshuvah*)
❖ Tishri 1 - *Yom Teruah* (first of 10 Days of Awe)
❖ Tishri 10 - *Yom Kippur* (Day of Atonement: 10th Day of Awe and 40th day of *Teshuvah*)

Notice that the Feast of Trumpets also initiates a time known in Hebrew as *yamim nora'im*, or "Days of Awe." The Days of Awe conclude with *Yom Kippur* - the Day of Atonement - making a total of ten days. It is believed that during this ten-day period, the "gates of heaven" are opened to hear the pentinent prayers of Israel. Judaism considers this season to be when the "fervent prayer of a righteous man" (Jas. 5:16) can potentially reverse any negative judgments made on *Yom Teruah*. The basis of this tradition rests partially on something the patriarch Jacob experienced.

"THEN HE DREAMED, AND BEHOLD, A LADDER WAS SET UP ON THE EARTH, AND ITS TOP REACHED TO HEAVEN; AND THERE THE ANGELS OF GOD WERE ASCENDING AND DESCENDING ON IT. AND BEHOLD, THE LORD STOOD ABOVE IT AND SAID, 'I AM THE LORD GOD OF ABRAHAM YOUR FATHER AND THE GOD OF ISAAC; THE LAND ON WHICH YOU LIE I WILL GIVE TO YOU AND YOUR DESCENDANTS. ALSO YOUR DESCENDANTS SHALL BE AS THE DUST OF THE EARTH; YOU SHALL SPREAD ABROAD TO THE WEST AND THE EAST, TO THE NORTH AND THE SOUTH; AND IN YOU AND IN YOUR SEED ALL THE FAMILIES OF THE EARTH SHALL BE BLESSED. BEHOLD, I AM WITH YOU AND WILL KEEP YOU WHEREVER YOU GO, AND WILL BRING YOU BACK TO THIS LAND; FOR I WILL NOT LEAVE YOU UNTIL I HAVE DONE WHAT I HAVE SPOKEN TO YOU.' THEN JACOB AWOKE FROM HIS SLEEP AND SAID, 'SURELY THE LORD IS IN THIS PLACE, AND I DID NOT KNOW IT.' AND HE WAS AFRAID AND SAID, 'HOW **AWESOME** IS THIS PLACE! THIS IS NONE OTHER THAN THE HOUSE OF GOD, AND THIS IS THE GATE OF HEAVEN!' " (GENESIS 28:12-17)

When Jacob described the place as being "awesome," he used the Hebrew word *norah*. This is the singular tense of the same word used to describe the Days of Awe - *nora'im* (the plural form of the word). So, we see the connection between the "awe-some days" and the opened "gates of heaven." Therefore, during the ten days of awe total repentance is critical because the gates of heaven are opened to those with repentant hearts. It is also believed that at the end of the ten days - which falls at the close of Yom Kippur - the gates of heaven will be shut. In fact, one of the last ceremonies of *Yom Kippur* is called *neilah* or "closing the gates."

It has become tradition that, when *neilah* is concluded, mankind is to accept that, what God has decreed during this season is sealed for the next twelve months. In other words, once it is decreed and sealed there is no chance of it being changed. This is one of the reasons this ten day period is regarded as "Days of Awe." Consequently, this season is regarded as a time of intense spiritual reflection and total repentance in advance of God's final decree for your life.

THE DECREE AGAINST NEBUCHADNEZZAR

To demonstrate the seriousness of God's decrees, let us consider what happened to the king of Babylon. History records that the city of Babylon was one of the greatest cities ever built by man. Her greatest and most famous king was, of course, Nebuchadnezzar. At the height of Babylon's glory King Nebuchadnezzar ruled over an unprecedented empire in terms of its geographical expanse, military might, and material wealth.

For example, according to C.M. Ward,

Nebuchadnezzar's banquet hall alone was over a mile long and measured over 1,600 feet in width. Enormous gold chains held equally large plants suspended over horseshoe-shaped tables. While seated at these tables, one could feast on the rarest of delicacies being served by trained peacocks. While dining one could listen to music supplied by multiple orchestras each of which numbered several thousand strong. Such was the glory of Nebuchadnezzar's Babylon.

Yet in a dream, Nebuchadnezzar was warned that, despite all his glory, he was going to be humbled (Dan. 4:10-18). Though he was likened to a tree whose height and breadth was unlike any other, he would nevertheless be cut down by a "watcher, a holy one." After being cut down, he would be given the heart of a beast for seven years. After that time had elapsed, he would realize his own weakness and acknowledge the greatness of the "Most High." Consequently, his kingdom would be restored to him. What I find to be the most fascinating aspect of this entire narrative is that Scripture says all of this was determined for Nebuchadnezzar by a ruling inspired by the "watchers."

"THIS DECISION IS BY THE DECREE OF THE WATCHERS, AND THE SENTENCE BY THE WORD OF THE HOLY ONES, IN ORDER THAT THE LIVING MAY KNOW THAT THE MOST HIGH RULES IN THE KINGDOM OF MEN, GIVES IT TO WHOMEVER HE WILL, AND SETS OVER IT THE LOWEST OF MEN."

(DANIEL 4:17)

In this passage, the word "decree" (Aramaic *bigzerat*) comes from a root word (Aramaic *gezar*) that means to "cut out." When making a judgment about a certain situation, certain conclusions must be "cut out" and set aside as the logical consequence of the situation. That conclusion is the decree. In this particular passage, this decree is made by "the watchers" who are also "holy ones." This is the only time the root word used here - *iyr* - is translated as "watcher." This word speaks of someone who has been awakened from slumber (maybe by the blast of a shofar?) and their eyes are made to see completely.

That they are also "holy ones" (Aramaic *kadishiyn*) implies that they are saints (the equivalent Hebrew word *kadoshim* is "set apart ones" or "saints.") In other words, it seems that certain saints of God - those who have been "set apart" by virtue of repentant and obedient hearts - began to cry out to the Father to intervene on their behalf. This prompted a heavenly investigation into Nebuchadnezzar's earthly deeds. This was, after all, the man who had ransacked the Holy Temple, removed its holy articles and carried God's people into captivity. After reviewing the evidence, a decision was made and the sentence carried out - according to the Bible, exactly one year later.

"At the end of the twelve months he was walking about the royal palace of Babylon. The king spoke, saying, 'Is not this great Babylon, that I have built for a royal dwelling by my mighty power and

FOR THE HONOR OF MY MAJESTY?' WHILE THE WORD WAS STILL IN THE KING'S MOUTH, A VOICE FELL FROM HEAVEN: 'KING NEBUCHADNEZZAR, TO YOU IT IS SPOKEN: THE KINGDOM HAS DEPARTED FROM YOU! AND THEY SHALL DRIVE YOU FROM MEN, AND YOUR DWELLING SHALL BE WITH THE BEASTS OF THE FIELD. THEY SHALL MAKE YOU EAT GRASS LIKE OXEN; AND SEVEN TIMES SHALL PASS OVER YOU, UNTIL YOU KNOW THAT THE MOST HIGH RULES IN THE KINGDOM OF MEN, AND GIVES IT TO WHOMEVER HE CHOOSES.' THAT VERY HOUR THE WORD WAS FULFILLED CONCERNING NEBUCHADNEZZAR; HE WAS DRIVEN FROM MEN AND ATE GRASS LIKE OXEN; HIS BODY WAS WET WITH THE DEW OF HEAVEN TILL HIS HAIR HAD GROWN LIKE EAGLES' FEATHERS AND HIS NAILS LIKE BIRDS' CLAWS." (DANIEL 4:29-33)

Understanding this example, there is reason to believe that the "holy ones" are qualified to petition God for an answer to prayer, or intervention on their behalf when they are under the thumb of the Oppressor. Furthermore, once a heavenly decision has been made, we have a biblical precedent which suggests the "decree" could come to fruition in just twelve months!

A LESSON FROM JOB

Job is one of the most fascinating narratives in the Scriptures. Here is a man who had everything - he was the greatest in the East (Job 1:3) - and then lost it all. He lost seven sons and three daughters to a storm (Job 1:2, 19). He lost seven thousand sheep when lightning hit them (Job 1:16). He had five hundred yoke of oxen as well as five hundred donkeys stolen (Job 1:14-15). On top of all this, he lost his health and the confidence of his wife (Job 2:7, 9). Yet, in the midst of all this trouble, Job declined to give up on God and die. To the contrary, he receives instructions in what to do so that his health and his wealth might be restored.

"If you return to the Almighty, you will be built up; you will remove iniquity far from your tents. Then you will lay your gold in the dust, and the gold of Ophir among the stones of the brooks. Yes, the Almighty will be your gold and your precious silver; for then you will have your delight in the Almighty, and lift up your face to God. You will make your prayer to Him, He will hear you, and you will pay your vows. You will also declare a thing, and it will be established for you; so light will shine on your ways." (Job 22:23-28)

Notice that righteous Job is told to perform specific tasks:

❖ "Return to the Almighty" - time of repentance.
❖ "Make your prayer to Him" - time of prayer.
❖ "Pay your vows" - time of giving.

After completing these tasks, he is told to "declare a thing." The word "declare" (*gazar*) is the

Hebrew equivalent of the Aramaic word, *gezar*, which used in Daniel for "decree." The "thing" being declared is the Hebrew word *omer*. This word comes from the Hebrew word *amar* and means "to speak", "to command." In other words, after repentance, prayer and paying vows, Job would be in an authoritative position to declare a command - to make a decree - and it would come to pass.

Notice that all of these points - repentance, prayer, giving offerings, and making decrees - are common to the Days of Awe. *Yom Teruah* is a time of repentance followed by a season of prayer. Offerings are given throughout this time and, finally, the decisions are sealed and decreed on *Yom Kippur*. It is obvious to me that this particular cycle - repentance, prayer, giving and decreeing - fits perfectly with the patterns that God has established in Scripture. It is also apparent that when we do what we are supposed to during these seasons, God will respond accordingly at the "appointed time."

MAY YOUR NAME BE INSCRIBED

The forty days of *teshuvah* is a time of year when observant Jews recognize the solemnity of the season and so, prepare themselves spiritually that he or she may be found worthy during this time of judgment. In acknowledgment of this desire to be deemed "worthy," certain customs have arisen which accentuate this point. One of the more interesting customs practiced during this time is the continued recitation of the 27th Psalm. In fact, it is recited beyond the Days of Repentance until the end of the Feast of Tabernacles. Taking this into consideration, I think it is important to include this Psalm in our study and meditate upon its meaning.

"THE LORD IS MY LIGHT AND MY SALVATION; WHOM SHALL I FEAR? THE LORD IS THE STRENGTH OF MY LIFE; OF WHOM SHALL I BE AFRAID? WHEN THE WICKED CAME AGAINST ME TO EAT UP MY FLESH, MY ENEMIES AND FOES, THEY STUMBLED AND FELL. THOUGH AN ARMY MAY ENCAMP AGAINST ME, MY HEART SHALL NOT FEAR; THOUGH WAR MAY RISE AGAINST ME, IN THIS I WILL BE CONFIDENT. ONE THING I HAVE DESIRED OF THE LORD, THAT WILL I SEEK: THAT I MAY DWELL IN THE HOUSE OF THE LORD ALL THE DAYS OF MY LIFE, TO BEHOLD THE BEAUTY OF THE LORD, AND TO INQUIRE IN HIS TEMPLE. FOR IN THE TIME OF TROUBLE HE SHALL HIDE ME IN HIS PAVILION; IN THE SECRET PLACE OF HIS TABERNACLE HE SHALL HIDE ME; HE SHALL SET ME HIGH UPON A ROCK. AND NOW MY HEAD SHALL BE LIFTED UP ABOVE MY ENEMIES ALL AROUND ME; THEREFORE I WILL OFFER SACRIFICES OF JOY IN HIS TABERNACLE; I WILL SING, YES, I WILL SING PRAISES TO THE LORD. HEAR, O LORD, WHEN I CRY WITH MY VOICE! HAVE MERCY ALSO UPON ME, AND ANSWER ME. WHEN YOU SAID, 'SEEK MY FACE,' MY HEART SAID TO YOU, 'YOUR FACE, LORD, I WILL SEEK.' DO NOT HIDE YOUR FACE FROM ME; DO NOT TURN YOUR SERVANT AWAY IN ANGER; YOU HAVE BEEN MY HELP; DO NOT LEAVE ME NOR FORSAKE ME, O GOD OF MY SALVATION. WHEN MY FATHER AND MY MOTHER FORSAKE ME, THEN THE

LORD WILL TAKE CARE OF ME. TEACH ME YOUR WAY, O LORD, AND LEAD ME IN A SMOOTH PATH, BECAUSE OF MY ENEMIES. DO NOT DELIVER ME TO THE WILL OF MY ADVERSARIES; FOR FALSE WITNESSES HAVE RISEN AGAINST ME, AND SUCH AS BREATHE OUT VIOLENCE. I WOULD HAVE LOST HEART, UNLESS I HAD BELIEVED THAT I WOULD SEE THE GOODNESS OF THE LORD IN THE LAND OF THE LIVING. WAIT ON THE LORD; BE OF GOOD COURAGE, AND HE SHALL STRENGTHEN YOUR HEART; WAIT, I SAY, ON THE LORD!"

(PSALM 27)

It is also customary at this time of year to remind your fellow believers of the need to prepare themselves during this time of repentance. Thus, a tradition evolved whereby someone, when corresponding with another, would include epithets such as: "Wishes for well being for the coming year," Other such salutations might include "Wishes for a good decision from the L-RD on Rosh Hashana," or "May your name be inscribed" (in the book of life).

It should be obvious that this "appointed time" is one for self-reflection of one's intents, deeds, conversations and every other aspect of life. It is the time for true repentance because it is also the time when names are inscribed or removed from the Book of Life. Interestingly, the New Testament hints at the validity of this view.

"HE WHO OVERCOMES SHALL BE CLOTHED IN WHITE GARMENTS, AND I WILL NOT BLOT OUT HIS NAME FROM THE BOOK OF LIFE; BUT I WILL CONFESS HIS NAME BEFORE MY

Father and before His angels." (Revelation 3:5)

"If anyone takes away from the words of the book of this prophecy, God shall take away his part from the Book of Life, from the holy city, and from the things which are written in this book."
(Revelation 22:19)

So then, what should we as believers glean from all of this? Is this all just something that God used to do under the so-called "Old" covenant? Has it been done away with? Or should we consider that God is not only eternal but eternally consistent? In other words, do the cycles and lessons we see in the Hebrew Scriptures still resonate in the 21st century? Should there be more soul searching, more prayer and more giving coming from believers in Jesus Christ during these appointed times? With all of my heart, I believe the answer to be "Yes!"

I have noticed in my own ministry that it was during this general time period when I experienced some of the greatest revivals as well as some of the greatest financial breakthroughs. I have noticed that direction for the ministry and answered prayer came primarily during the fall months. I never understood the significance of this until I understood the seasons of God and **when** He makes decrees.

So then, I ask you: "What do you need from God in the next twelve months?" Do you want to see your unsaved family members moved with conviction? Do you need a miracle in your life? How about a breakthrough in your business or in your marriage? Are you willing to subject your will to the Will of the Father? Are you prepared to follow the lessons and pattern that He has established? Friends, there is an appointed time to repent, an ordained season to pray, and a specific time to petition Heaven. Furthermore, when we follow God's ways and patterns, there will be, as a result, times of refreshing!

Chapter Four

TIMES OF REFRESHING AND RESTORATION

"REPENT THEREFORE AND BE CONVERTED, THAT YOUR SINS MAY BE BLOTTED OUT, SO THAT TIMES OF REFRESHING MAY COME FROM THE PRESENCE OF THE LORD, AND THAT HE MAY SEND JESUS CHRIST, WHO WAS PREACHED TO YOU BEFORE, WHOM HEAVEN MUST RECEIVE UNTIL THE TIMES OF RESTORATION OF ALL THINGS, WHICH GOD HAS SPOKEN BY THE MOUTH OF ALL HIS HOLY PROPHETS SINCE THE WORLD BEGAN." (ACTS 3:19-21)

In the Hebrew Scriptures, when God's people repented, the typical result was the blessing of rain upon their fields, crops and vineyards. This fruitfulness led to further restoration and prosperity. In the New Testament when repentance was evident, prayers were answered and people were released from various bondages. This spiritual refreshing is likened to the rainy season of old - even as the rain refreshes, likewise, the rain of the Holy Spirit is intended to send refreshing to those whose hearts are intent on returning to the Lord. It seems then, that the season of repentance is the prelude to a season of refreshing.

In Acts 3, the word translated as "refreshing" is the Greek word *anapsuxis* and means literally, "a recovery of breath." It is intended to infer that someone who has lost his breath and has fainted from exhaustion is suddenly renewed and revived when the breath is recovered. Our modern word "revival" conveys the same idea. Thus, we are to understand that Peter spoke of a revival and refreshing that would come from the presence of the Lord, **after people repented**! Today, when there is true and heart-felt repentance, there indeed comes a time of refreshing and revival.

If repentance is the prelude to refreshing, then the refreshing comes as the introduction to complete restoration. In Acts 3, we are promised that "all things" will be restored. Of course, this is specifically dealing with the advent of the Messianic age when Jesus Christ rules and reigns from Jerusalem. Nevertheless, "all" means "all" and that has to imply that when God's people repent, they will be refreshed - rained upon - and will experience complete restoration, ultimately personified by the Messianic era. The epistle of James puts it this way:

"Therefore be patient, brethren, until the coming of the Lord. See how the farmer waits for

THE PRECIOUS FRUIT OF THE EARTH, WAITING PATIENTLY FOR IT UNTIL IT RECEIVES THE EARLY AND LATTER RAIN. YOU ALSO BE PATIENT. ESTABLISH YOUR HEARTS, FOR THE COMING OF THE LORD IS AT HAND." (JAMES 5:7-8)

In the days of the Temple, the Feast of Tabernacles was also considered to be the Feast of the Ingathering. This was symbolized by the ingathering of the fruits of trees and the field which were brought up to Jerusalem. In fact, seven different fruits were gathered in a basket, the basket placed between the horns of an ox which was led into the Temple courtyards.

It is understood that these seven fruits were to symbolize fruit coming from all seven continents. In other words, this was to signify that, in the end, God would have worshippers coming up to Jerusalem to extol Him from every nation on earth. You see, *Sukkot* or Tabernacles was the feast that acknowledged the ingathering of Jews and not Jews only, but:

"...ALSO THAT HE WOULD GATHER TOGETHER IN ONE THE CHILDREN OF GOD WHO WERE SCATTERED ABROAD."
(JOHN 11:52)

Those "scattered abroad" is intended to mean all of those living among the Gentiles. Scripture tells us that during the Millennial reign of Messiah, all nations shall go up to Jerusalem to worship the King at the Feast of Tabernacles (Zech. 14:16). Furthermore, those who do not will not receive the rain which is needed to produce the fruit (Zech. 14:18-19) represented at Tabernacles. At any rate, we see that Tabernacles represents the refreshing and total restoration that begins with the repentance begun during the season of *teshuvah.*

At this point we need to understand that the common denominator of both repentance and restoration is the Word of God. What I mean by that is, to truly repent is to return to God, His ways and His Word! The restoration of all things - as spoken by all of His holy prophets since the world began - is when the world returns to His Word and His ways under the kingship of the Messiah. Thus, the Scripture records that:

"MANY PEOPLE SHALL COME AND SAY, 'COME AND LET US GO UP TO THE MOUNTAIN OF THE LORD, TO THE HOUSE OF THE GOD OF JACOB. HE WILL TEACH US HIS WAYS, AND WE SHALL WALK IN HIS PATHS.' FOR OUT OF ZION SHALL GO FORTH THE LAW (THE TORAH), AND THE WORD OF THE LORD FROM JERUSALEM." (ISAIAH 2:3)

This is the ultimate meaning of the restoration of "all things" and thus we see that returning to God - repentance - is equivalent to returning to His ways as defined by Scripture. In the Scripture, His ways are demonstrated for us through His cycles and His "appointed times." In the appointed time He will restore all things through and by His Word personified by the Messiah Jesus. It is He who will sit upon the throne of David in Jerusalem and "rule all nations with a rod of iron" (Rev. 12: 5).

The point of this is, that rod of iron is intended to bring all nations under subjection to the Word of God. As His people, we should not require a rod to bring us under subjection to the Word; we should do so because we love Him. That love should prompt a desire to understand His ways and the only way to do that is to understand His Word - all of it. When we do - when we follow God's ways and according to His appointed times - then we will experience abundant life. Jesus, the Living Word said:

"I HAVE COME THAT THEY MAY HAVE LIFE, AND THAT THEY MAY HAVE IT MORE ABUNDANTLY." (JOHN 10:10)

DAYS OF JOY

Abundant living is synonymous with being happy and full of joy. Following the ten Days of Awe and the ominous nature of *Yom Kippur* comes the joy and celebration of the Feast of Tabernacles. Tabernacles or "booths" is a time that is to acknowledge God's Presence among His people. It looks back upon the time when God provided food, water, shelter and protection for Israel while in the wilderness. It looks forward to the day when the Messiah will "tabernacle" among us and will again be the sole source of our every need. In short, it is the Feast of the Kingdom - when **all** things are restored.

In the Second Temple era, the last day or eighth day (*Shemini Atzeret*) of *Sukkot* was considered to be the close of the feast (Num. 29:35). As a result, this day was regarded as a time to tarry and spend intimate time with the Almighty. This day was also highlighted by one of the richest and most joyous images of the feast - the water libation ceremony. This ritual, which was performed on the night beginning this eighth day (a Hebrew day begins at twilight), was symbolic of fruitfulness - a time to pray for rain in the next growing season. One of the prayers during this time was taken from Psalm 118 and entreated the Lord thus:

"SAVE NOW, I PRAY, O LORD, O LORD, I PRAY, SEND NOW PROSPERITY." (PSALM 118:25)

As I related earlier, this ceremony was apparently occurring when Jesus stood up and spoke during the feast of Tabernacles.

"ON THE LAST DAY, THAT GREAT DAY OF THE FEAST, JESUS STOOD AND CRIED OUT, SAYING, 'IF ANYONE THIRSTS, LET HIM COME TO ME AND DRINK. HE WHO BELIEVES IN ME, AS THE SCRIPTURE HAS SAID, OUT OF HIS HEART WILL FLOW RIVERS OF LIVING WATER. BUT THIS HE SPOKE CONCERNING THE SPIRIT, WHOM THOSE BELIEVING IN HIM WOULD RECEIVE; FOR THE HOLY SPIRIT WAS NOT YET GIVEN, BECAUSE JESUS WAS NOT YET GLORIFIED."
(JOHN 7:37-39)

On the day following this ceremony and Jesus' dramatic declaration, a women caught in adultery was brought before Jesus.

"AND WHEN THEY HAD SET HER IN THE MIDST, THEY
SAID TO HIM, 'TEACHER, THIS WOMAN WAS CAUGHT IN ADUL-
TERY, IN THE VERY ACT. NOW MOSES, IN THE LAW, COM-
MANDED US THAT SUCH SHOULD BE STONED. BUT WHAT DO
YOU SAY?' THIS THEY SAID, TESTING HIM, THAT THEY MIGHT
HAVE SOMETHING OF WHICH TO ACCUSE HIM. BUT JESUS
STOOPED DOWN AND WROTE ON THE GROUND WITH HIS FIN-
GER, AS THOUGH HE DID NOT HEAR. SO WHEN THEY CON-
TINUED ASKING HIM, HE RAISED HIMSELF UP AND SAID TO
THEM, 'HE WHO IS WITHOUT SIN AMONG YOU, LET HIM THROW
A STONE AT HER FIRST.' AND AGAIN HE STOOPED DOWN AND
WROTE ON THE GROUND. THEN THOSE WHO HEARD IT, BEING
CONVICTED BY THEIR CONSCIENCE, WENT OUT ONE BY ONE,
BEGINNING WITH THE OLDEST EVEN TO THE LAST. AND JESUS
WAS LEFT ALONE, AND THE WOMAN STANDING IN THE MIDST.
WHEN JESUS HAD RAISED HIMSELF UP AND SAW NO ONE
BUT THE WOMAN, HE SAID TO HER, 'WOMAN, WHERE ARE
THOSE ACCUSERS OF YOURS? HAS NO ONE CONDEMNED
YOU?' SHE SAID, 'NO ONE LORD." AND JESUS SAID TO HER,
'NEITHER DO I CONDEMN YOU. GO AND SIN NO MORE.' "
(JOHN 8:3-11)

This is a fascinating account, not just because
of the outcome, but because of the timing of the outcome. In other words, that it took place during a particular appointed time at which the Messiah had pro-
claimed Himself to be the "living water" is not coincidental. Now, a lot of speculation has arisen over the
years as to what Jesus was writing in the dust. When

you consider what time of year this was and then realize that one of the Scripture readings for the Feast of *Sukkot* was taken from Jeremiah 17, the mystery begins to clear.

"O LORD, THE HOPE OF ISRAEL; ALL WHO FORSAKE YOU SHALL BE ASHAMED. THOSE WHO DEPART FROM ME SHALL BE WRITTEN IN THE EARTH, BECAUSE THEY HAVE FORSAKEN THE LORD, THE **FOUNTAIN OF LIVING WATERS**."
(JEREMIAH 17:13)

That He was writing in the dust should be evidence enough of what He was trying to prove. Still, it is important to understand what was supposed to happen to a woman accused of adultery. According to the Torah (Numbers 5:11-31), such a woman was to be brought before a priest. The priest would take holy water - understood to be *mayim chayim* or "living water" - in an earthen vessel and mix it with dust taken from the floor of the tabernacle or temple.

With the grain offering for jealousy in her hand and standing before the Lord with her head uncovered, the priest would write curses in a book and scrape them off into the vessel which contained the water. Thus, this water became "bitter water that brings a curse." She would then be compelled to drink the water. If she were guilty, her belly would swell, her thigh would rot and she would be considered a curse among her people.

This is what the woman in John 8 was facing, except her accusers meant to use her to go after bigger prey - Jesus. Perhaps their attempt was fueled by what had happened the night before when He claimed to be the living water. Whatever their motivation might have been, they didn't obtain their objective. Instead of snaring Him, they were the ones ensnared, for the dust that would have been used to condemn the woman was used to condemn them instead. Why? Because these men had obviously "forsaken the Lord, the fountain of living waters."

Please keep in mind that this occurred on the Eighth Day - *shemini atzeret*. On this day there was great celebration and overflowing joy. It was also the day Israel anticipated rain for a **fruitful** future. It should then be noted that a woman deemed "not guilty" by the test of bitter waters was considered "free" and eligible to "conceive children" (Num. 5:28) or in other words, to be **fruitful**. When the woman caught in adultery left the Presence of the Messiah, she was **refreshed and restored** and free to be fruitful - all on the eighth day! There is no doubt in my mind that she left **rejoicing** in the Lord.

It just so happens that the eighth day of the Feast is also called *Simchat Torah* or "Rejoicing in the Torah (Word)." This is when observant Jews dance with the Torah Scroll which has been rolled (restored) all the way back to the beginning of Genesis. It is a time of rejoicing, a time of refreshing that has followed a time of repentance. Once again, this speaks of total restoration that we will experience in the Kingdom. You see, we all are like the adulterous woman - deserving of death. Yet, the One who is the Living

Water placed in an earthen vessel, the One who is the Living Torah has:

"REDEEMED US FROM THE CURSE OF THE LAW, HAVING BECOME A CURSE FOR US." (GALATIANS 3:13)

He has made it possible that we who have been restored can also rejoice along with the woman of John 8 in the Kingdom. There, we will rejoice in the Living Word, the Messiah. The Millennial reign of Christ will truly be a time of "refreshing" and the time of the "restoration of all things." Yet, the lesson and nature of Tabernacles - the season of joy and refreshing - can be realized today if we understand and apply to our lives the principles inherent in God's appointed times.

SEASONS OF ANSWERED PRAYER

Each day there is a set time when God's Presence is exceptionally strong. In the Temple period, the early morning was when the Holy Menorah was renewed with fresh oil. Early morning prayers were offered as well as the burning of incense (Ex. 30:7) and the offerings of a lamb (Ex. 29:39). Jews have long believed that the early morning hours is when God's Presence is roaming throughout the world and when He is most readily received by men.

If you recall, it was during these early morning hours that Christ would often pray (Mt. 14:25). Apparently, Jesus wasn't the only one who believed in rising early in order to meet with God. The Scripture records that Abraham rose early (Gen. 19:27) as did Jacob (Gen. 28:18), Moses (Ex. 8:20), Joshua (Jos. 3:1), Samuel (1 Sam. 15:12), and David (1 Sam. 17:20). It seems that these men understood that there was a particular time when to pray and make their petition known to God.

I believe that God hears prayers at all hours and at all times. Furthermore, I believe that He answers prayers at all times. However, it is obvious that there are pre-appointed seasons of favor when He releases blessings and answers our prayers. Consider the following:

"AND IT SHALL BE THAT IF YOU EARNESTLY OBEY MY COMMANDMENTS WHICH I COMMAND YOU TODAY, TO LOVE THE LORD YOU GOD AND SERVE HIM WITH ALL YOUR HEART AND WITH ALL YOUR SOUL, THEN I WILL GIVE YOU THE RAIN FOR YOUR LAND IN ITS SEASON, THE EARLY RAIN AND THE LATTER RAIN, THAT YOU MAY GATHER IN YOUR GRAIN, YOUR NEW WINE, AND YOUR OIL." (DEUTERONOMY 11:13-14)

The Lord makes it clear that if we do what we are supposed to - that is, to love and obey Him (do **what** He says **when** He says) - then, **when it is the season**, He will release the blessings we need in order to prosper. So then, if we do what we are instructed to do during the days of *Teshuvah*, and truly return to God with all of our hearts, then during the subsequent days of refreshing, we will witness a season of answered prayer unlike any other. Again, this is not to say that prayers are to be prayed during this time exclusively. No, prayer can and should be offered all the time. Consider the prophet Daniel who was given an answer after a twenty-one day fast.

"Do not fear, Daniel, for from the first day that you set your heart to understand, and to humble yourself before your God, your words were heard; and I have come because of your words."
(Daniel 10:12)

So, we see that God is willing to answer sincere prayers at any time. Still, we must understand that there are times God considers special and, consequently, special things happen during these appointed times. I suggest to you that, if you spend time with God during the season of repentance, He will visit you with a season of refreshing and restoration. Contemplate, therefore, what you are willing to do to see to it that this time of refreshing occurs in your life. Are you prepared to turn to Him with all of your heart? Is there anything that you would hold back from Him? I believe that, as we turn to Him, we must be willing to offer to Him from our hearts and our resources.

Chapter Five

SEASONS OF GIVING

"BRING ALL THE TITHES INTO THE STOREHOUSE, THAT THERE MAY BE FOOD IN MY HOUSE, AND TRY ME NOW IN THIS, SAYS THE LORD OF HOSTS, IF I WILL NOT OPEN FOR YOU THE WINDOWS OF HEAVEN AND POUR OUT FOR YOU SUCH BLESSING THAT THERE WILL NOT BE ROOM ENOUGH TO RECEIVE IT." (MALACHI 3:10)

During the days of the Temple, there were many types of offerings to be given at certain times and for specific reasons. For our purposes I want to point out five primary offerings that were presented unto the Lord. First there was the *minchah,* sometimes called in the Scripture "meat-offering," or "meal offering." This offering generally consisted of things without life (i.e. ears of corn, flour, grain, oil). This was often given with the intent of thanking God and acknowledging Him for the fruit of our labors.

Another significant offering is the *olah* or "burnt offering." *Olah*, from *alah*, means "to ascend" because this offering, being wholly consumed, ascended to God in smoke. The whole burnt offering was given to God expressing the person's willingness to offer nothing less than complete and total submission to Him and to His will. Paul exhorts us to be this type of servant when he says:

"I BESEECH YOU THEREFORE, BRETHREN, BY THE MERCIES OF GOD, THAT YOU PRESENT YOUR BODIES A LIVING SACRIFICE, HOLY, ACCEPTABLE TO GOD, WHICH IS YOUR REASONABLE SERVICE." (ROMANS 12:1)

The "trespass offering," or *asham*, speaks of one who is "guilty," or "liable to punishment." When the giver presented this sacrifice, his guilt was considered as being transferred to the animal offered to God. Consequently, the guilty was redeemed from the penalty of his sin. Although not exclusively, this was typically offered when someone had transgressed against his fellow man.

The *chattat*, "sin offering," comes from the word *chata*, or "to miss the mark." Although it signifies sin in general, it is more often used when someone has sinned against God. The sin offering was presented in acknowledgment of the offender's desire to return to God, knowing that to do so required the shedding of innocent blood. In this, we truly see the significance of what Christ performed on our behalf. Perhaps this is what Paul had in mind when he wrote:

"FOR HE MADE HIM WHO KNEW NO SIN TO BE SIN FOR US, THAT WE MIGHT BECOME THE RIGHTEOUSNESS OF GOD IN HIM." (2 CORINTHIANS 5:21)

The *shalamim*, or peace offering, comes from the word *shalam*. This word means "to complete, make whole." Of course, this is where the word *shalom* comes from. This offering was to make up for anything that might be considered lacking by any of the previous offerings. The covenant of God, broken by His people, was supposed to be made whole; so that after such an offering, the sincere and humble man had confidence to accept that the breach between he and God had been repaired. The former transgressor could then be at peace. Paul obviously alludes to this in his letter to the Ephesians.

"FOR HE HIMSELF IS OUR PEACE, WHO HAS MADE BOTH ONE, AND HAS BROKEN DOWN THE MIDDLE WALL OF SEPARATION, HAVING ABOLISHED IN HIS FLESH THE ENMITY, THAT IS, THE LAW OF COMMANDMENTS CONTAINED IN ORDI-NANCES, SO AS TO CREATE IN HIMSELF ONE NEW MAN FROM THE TWO, THUS MAKING PEACE, AND THAT HE MIGHT REC-ONCILE THEM BOTH TO GOD IN ONE BODY THROUGH THE CROSS, THEREBY PUTTING TO DEATH THE ENMITY."
(EPHESIANS 2:14-16)

Even with all of these offerings, each intended for specific purposes, it was understood in antiquity that Israel did not have to wait for any particular day in order to repent before God. We see evidence of this when David, confronted with his sin by Nathan the prophet, immediately confessed and repented (2 Sam. 12). Likewise, you and I should never hesitate to repent to the Lord when we are made aware of our shortcomings. Nevertheless, God did establish a season when His nation was to come together to reflect and repent of their sins so the favor of God would be upon them throughout the year. That season, of course, was the days of *Teshuvah* culminating with *Yom Kippur.*

So, considering that there are special times when our actions can solicit a unique response from heaven, it stands to reason that the cause and effect of giving specific offerings during particular seasons can bring about unique results as well. In other words is it possible that, at the time when the **ears** of heaven are most attuned to our prayers, the **eyes** of heaven are most attentive of our offerings? Consider the account of the Roman centurion Cornelius.

"There was a certain man in Caesarea called Cornelius, a centurion of what was called the Italian Regiment, a devout man and one who feared God with all his household, who gave alms generously to the people, and prayed to God always. About the ninth hour of the day he saw clearly in a vision an angel of God coming in and saying to him, 'Cornelius!' And when he observed him, he was afraid, and said, 'What is it, Lord?' So he said to him, 'Your prayers and your alms have come up for a memorial before God.' "

(Acts 10:1-4)

After much prayer and apparent giving, Cornelius was told, his prayers and alms had come up for a "memorial" before God (Acts 10:4). Our understanding of memorial is something of "record" or a "reminder" or "memorandum." If someone told you that you have a meeting next week, you would probably write it down somewhere so that you would be sure to keep the date. It would be a memorial.

Obviously Cornelius' sincere prayers and heart-felt giving had placed his name on God's record for future recognition. Understanding that miraculous events do occur during certain seasons it seems that when the appointed time for Cornelius arrived, he was situated to receive his due - God would remember him because of his prayer and his giving.

From a Hebraic point of view, a "memorial" or "to remember" means much more than what we think of in the West. The word zikron, translated as "memorial" means "a memorable thing," "a day" or "a writing." This word expresses that "something is written to remind someone to do something on a certain day." To some degree, that sounds a lot like our meaning of the word. However, when we look at the root word zakar, the true intent of the word makes a deeper impression. Zakar, translated as "remembrance," means "to mark" something. The "mark," it is inferred, comes by "burning" something - as in an offering.

Those meanings are very interesting, nevertheless, the purest and most astounding meaning of the word zakar is "to speak on behalf" of someone. For instance, when Nehemiah was restoring the

Temple, he asked God to:

> "REMEMBER ME, MY GOD, FOR GOOD, ACCORDING
> TO ALL THAT I HAVE DONE FOR THIS PEOPLE."
> (NEHEMIAH 5:19)

In reality, he was asking God to take note of what he had done and then "Speak on my behalf."

When God "remembered Noah" (Gen. 8:1), the Scripture wasn't inferring that God had forgotten him. No, the text is saying that, due to Noah's obedience, it had come time for God to speak on his behalf. When He began to speak up for Noah, the flood waters began to abate. Oddly enough, the day on which Noah removed the cover of the ark and discovered that the surface of the ground was dry was "in the first month, the first day of the month." More than likely, this was referring to the older calendar - before Exodus 12 - and therefore would have been the day which later became *Yom Teruah* or the Feast of Trumpets. So then, God had begun to speak on Noah's behalf during a season that led up to what would become the feast of Trumpets.

Having this information, we should more fully understand that when we walk according to God's statutes, when we give of ourselves and our resources for the benefit of God's purposes, and when we do these things during His appointed times, He will "mark" us for a blessing. He will speak on our behalf. When will He do this? At the appointed time - a time He has already determined - is when God "remembers" you and me and speaks on our behalf. It is interesting to note that the Feast of Trumpets is also called the "Day of Remembrance." At that time, so it is believed, the "Book of Remembrance" is opened in heaven.

THE BOOKS IN HEAVEN

In the book of Daniel, it was stipulated that his book must be sealed up until the time of the end (Dan. 12:9) In Revelation we see that John's book must remain unsealed (Rev. 22:10). The prophet Daniel as well as the Book of Revelation refer to other books being opened in Heaven (Dan. 7:10, Rev. 20:12). Other scriptures recognize the existence of other books - sealed and unsealed - that you and I can't read. Why? These books are apparently only read by God Himself.

In regard to all of these books, it is understood that God reviews them, placing names, omitting names or, depending on what is written in them, passing decrees where life and death may very well hang in the balance. In fact, Judaism believes that when these heavenly books are opened three groups are being examined and judged. They are:

- ❖ The totally righteous whose names are inscribed.
- ❖ The totally unrighteous whose names are blotted out.

❖ Those who are neither totally righteous or totally unrighteous, who must decide.

I wish to briefly mention some of the books beginning with the "Book of the Living," also called the "Book of Destiny" by the Jews

"LET THEM BE BLOTTED OUT OF THE BOOK OF THE LIVING, AND NOT BE WRITTEN WITH THE RIGHTEOUS."
(PSALM 69:28)

"YOUR EYES SAW MY SUBSTANCE, BEING YET UNFORMED. AND IN YOUR BOOK THEY ALL WERE WRITTEN, THE DAYS FASHIONED FOR ME, WHEN AS YET THERE WERE NONE OF THEM." (PSALM 139:16)

The Amplified Version of the Scriptures states it this way:

"YOUR EYES SAW MY UNFORMED SUBSTANCE, AND IN YOUR BOOK ALL THE DAYS OF MY LIFE WERE WRITTEN BEFORE EVER THEY TOOK SHAPE, WHEN AS YET THERE WAS NONE OF THEM." (PSALM 139:16) AMP

The Bible tells us there is a "Book of Tears."

"YOU NUMBER MY WANDERINGS; PUT MY TEARS INTO YOUR BOTTLE; ARE THEY NOT IN YOUR BOOK?"
(PSALM 56:8)

The New Testament reveals that there are

"books" and most notably, the "Lamb's Book of Life."

"HE WHO OVERCOMES SHALL BE CLOTHED IN WHITE GARMENTS, AND I WILL NOT BLOT OUT HIS NAME FROM THE BOOK OF LIFE; BUT I WILL CONFESS HIS NAME BEFORE MY FATHER AND BEFORE HIS ANGELS." (REVELATION 3:5)

"AND I SAW THE DEAD, SMALL AND GREAT, STANDING BEFORE GOD, AND BOOKS WERE OPENED. AND ANOTHER BOOK WAS OPENED, WHICH IS THE BOOK OF LIFE. AND THE DEAD WERE JUDGED ACCORDING TO THEIR WORKS, BY THE THINGS WHICH WERE WRITTEN IN THE BOOKS."
(REVELATION 20:12)

One of the most intriguing of these heavenly books is the "Book of Remembrance."

"AND I WILL REBUKE THE DEVOURER FOR YOUR SAKES, SO THAT HE WILL NOT DESTROY THE FRUIT OF YOUR GROUND, NOR SHALL THE VINE FAIL TO BEAR FRUIT FOR YOU IN THE FIELD, SAYS THE LORD OF HOSTS; AND ALL NATIONS WILL CALL YOU BLESSED, FOR YOU WILL BE A DELIGHTFUL LAND, SAYS THE LORD OF HOSTS. YOUR WORDS HAVE BEEN HARSH AGAINST ME, SAYS THE LORD, YET YOU SAY, 'WHAT HAVE WE SPOKEN AGAINST YOU?' YOU HAVE SAID, 'IT IS USELESS TO SERVE GOD; WHAT PROFIT IS IT THAT WE HAVE KEPT HIS ORDINANCE, AND THAT WE HAVE WALKED AS MOURNERS BEFORE THE LORD OF HOSTS? SO NOW WE CALL THE PROUD BLESSED, FOR THOSE WHO DO WICKED-NESS ARE RAISED UP; THEY EVEN TEMPT GOD AND GO FREE.' THEN THOSE WHO FEARED THE LORD SPOKE TO ONE

ANOTHER, AND THE LORD LISTENED AND HEARD THEM; SO A BOOK OF REMEMBRANCE WAS WRITTEN BEFORE HIM FOR THOSE WHO FEAR THE LORD AND WHO MEDITATE ON HIS NAME. THEY SHALL BE MINE, SAYS THE LORD OF HOSTS, ON THE DAY THAT I MAKE THEM MY JEWELS. AND I WILL SPARE THEM AS A MAN SPARES HIS OWN SON WHO SERVES HIM. THEN YOU SHALL AGAIN DISCERN BETWEEN THE RIGHTEOUS AND THE WICKED, BETWEEN ONE WHO SERVES GOD AND ONE WHO DOES NOT SERVE HIM." MALACHI 3:11-18

To understand the purpose of this book it is important to understand what is going on in the background. The Jews had returned from captivity and were spending a lot of time and money investing in themselves. As a result, the Temple of God was being ignored and forsaken. Into this situation steps the prophet Malachi to rebuke the people, specifically addressing their failure to bring "tithes and offerings."

"WILL A MAN ROB GOD? YET YOU HAVE ROBBED ME! BUT YOU SAY, 'IN WHAT WAY HAVE WE ROBBED YOU?' IN TITHES AND OFFERINGS. YOU ARE CURSED WITH A CURSE, FOR YOU HAVE ROBBED ME, EVEN THIS WHOLE NATION. BRING ALL THE TITHES INTO THE STOREHOUSE, THAT THERE MAY BE FOOD IN MY HOUSE, AND TRY ME NOW IN THIS, SAYS THE LORD OF HOSTS, IF I WILL NOT OPEN FOR YOU THE WINDOWS OF HEAVEN AND POUR OUT FOR YOU SUCH BLESSING THAT THERE WILL NOT BE ROOM ENOUGH TO RECEIVE IT. AND I WILL REBUKE THE DEVOURER FOR YOUR SAKES, SO THAT HE WILL NOT DESTROY THE FRUIT OF YOUR GROUND, NOR SHALL THE VINE FAIL TO BEAR FRUIT FOR YOU IN THE

FIELD, SAYS THE LORD OF HOSTS." (MALACHI 3:8-11)

It does not seem coincidental that in the same chapter, Malachi speaks both of the people's lack of giving, their wickedness and a book which records the names of those who remain faithful. It is implied then, that those who remember the House of God will be written in God's "Book of Remembrance." Those that fear the Lord have the promise that God will "remember" them - that is, at the proper time, He will speak on their behalf! When we consider the account in Acts 10 concerning Cornelius, I believe we have an example of when this book is opened and how it works.

First of all, remember that Cornelius feared God. Scripture tells us that:

"THE FEAR OF THE LORD IS THE BEGINNING OF WISDOM. (PSALM 111:10)

Also, He prayed continually inferring that God was inclined to listen to His prayers and move on his behalf (Jas. 5:16). That he gave alms, suggests that he cared for and gave to the poor and needy. Finally, his giving coupled with his prayers came up for a memorial. You might ask, "How does prayer come up?" In the Bible we are told that the prayers in the Temple "went up" from the altar of incense (Ps. 141:2). We also understand that prayers are kept in golden vials in the heavenly Temple (Rev. 5:8). When the vials are opened the "words come up before God." Where giving is concerned, the Scripture records that:

"Here mortal men receive tithes, but there he receives them, of whom it is witnessed that he lives."
(Hebrews 7:8)

All of this came up for a memorial and God moved on Cornelius' behalf, presumably because the centurion had been written in the "Book of Remembrance."

Now, consider that the season of *teshuvah* - a time God's people should turn to Him with their whole hearts - is linked to the Day of Remembrance or the feast of Trumpets. This is the day when God is prepared to speak on behalf of those who have repented, those who have prayed, and those who have given of their resources. Remember that on this day, the shofar is sounded repeatedly and the "voice" of the shofar is likened to the "voice of God." When God speaks, lives are changed.

Taking this all into account, should we not be motivated to prepare ourselves even now for what is expected of us? Furthermore, shouldn't we prepare our hearts now in anticipation of what we desire for the Father to decree for us in the next year?

Open The Windows of Heaven

Throughout the Scripture, we see that there are openings into heaven and, at times, these apertures are opened for us. Jesus once referred to heaven being "opened" and "angels ascending" (Jn. 1:51). In Revelation, John saw a door in heaven open (Rev.

4:1) and later saw heaven opened (Rev. 19:11). When these "doors" and "windows" are opened, what does it mean for us? Based on what Malachi wrote in chapter 3, it seems that an open heaven implies that blessings are going to rain down upon God's people.

The word translated as "windows" in Malachi 3:10 is *arubot*. The root word is *arubah*. Some translations, like the NIV, incorrectly interpret this word as "flood gates." On the contrary, the word *arubah* conveys the image of something akin to a pigeon hole or chimney. These would be relatively small openings, but nevertheless, sufficient to serve their purpose. The purpose, in this case, is to pour out blessings from heaven to earth but focused on those who have been faithful to God.

The word *arubah* also implies a lattice, which is connected to the idea of someone watching another through a very small opening. They are peering through the lattice, gathering information in order to do something that involves the person they are looking at. This imagery suggests that God observes our actions through the lattice "window," waiting for the right season to open the window and bestow a blessing upon us. Would you like to live under one of these windows from which unlimited blessing is poured out? This is what God told Malachi He would do for those who are faithful to give into His house.

This idea of an open window also connects back to something I referred to earlier and that is the "gate of heaven" that Jacob saw in Bethel. Recall that Jacob was in fear for his life and was fleeing from

Esau, so you might say, he needed to hear from God. On his flight into Syria - which would last for twenty years - he decided to stop in a place that was then called Luz to rest for the night. While he was sleeping he dreamed of a staircase upon which angels were ascending and descending between heaven and earth. At the top of this staircase stood the Lord who promised him and his descendants the land on which he lay (Gen. 28: 13). He also promised that through his seed, all the families of the earth would be blessed (Gen. 28:14).

When Jacob awoke he determined that he had been sleeping very near to the "gate of heaven" and the house of God (Gen. 28:17). On the next morning he took the stone which had been at his head and set it up as a pillar and anointed it with oil. This is understood to mean that he was establishing a **memorial**. It is then that Jacob made a vow.

The Bible records that Jacob renamed this place "Bethel," or "house of God. The former name, Luz, meant "an almond tree." By renaming it to the "house of God" demonstrated his belief that "surely the Lord is in this place" (Gen. 28:16). Furthermore, "Bethel" attested to the fact that this place was where the windows of heaven were opened,

According to the late Rabbi Yehudah Getz, there were actually two Bethels and this particular one was what became known later as the Temple Mount in Jerusalem. It was the same place that Abraham had been led to in order to offer Isaac as an *olah* or "burnt offering" (Gen. 22:2). Actually, the Scripture refers to this spot at "the place," or in Hebrew *ha makom.* According to rabbinic sources *ha Makom* is understood as being "the Lord." So, in other words Abraham took Isaac to the place where the Lord is seen (Gen. 22:14).

The *Book of Jasher* confirms that "The place" of Genesis 22 is the same place where Jacob saw the "gate of heaven" opened.

"AND JACOB WENT FORTH CONTINUING HIS ROAD TO HARAN, AND HE CAME AS FAR AS MOUNT MORIAH, AND HE TARRIED THERE ALL NIGHT NEAR A CITY NAMED LUZ; AND THE LORD APPEARED THERE UNTO JACOB ON THAT NIGHT."

(JASHER 30:1)

The point I wish to make here is, the "gate of heaven" is a place where blessings were poured out onto God's people through this open window. But don't miss this point either; it is also the place where God's people offered their sacrifices and prayerful petitions. Below are a few examples of what took place here.

- ❖ Where Abraham paid tithe (Gen. 14).
- ❖ Where Abraham took Isaac (Gen. 22).
- ❖ Isaac took Rebecca to Moriah to pray for child (Jasher 26:5).
- ❖ Jacob saw the vision of the ladder (Gen. 28).
- ❖ Site of the future temple built by Solomon.
- ❖ The Second Temple also stood on this site.

❖ Where sacrifices would be made and where offerings would be received.

Mt. Moriah is where all these things occurred and where angels had been seen descending and ascending between heaven and earth. Presumably, the angelic activity here is to demonstrate how the offerings made by mankind are taken to God, and how God's answer and blessing is bestowed upon man. Understanding this, notice what Jacob did on the morning after his dream.

"THEN JACOB MADE A VOW, SAYING, 'IF GOD WILL BE WITH ME, AND KEEP ME IN THIS WAY THAT I AM GOING, AND GIVE ME BREAD TO EAT AND CLOTHING TO PUT ON, SO THAT I COME BACK TO MY FATHER'S HOUSE IN PEACE, THEN THE LORD SHALL BE MY GOD. AND THIS STONE WHICH I HAVE SET AS A PILLAR SHALL BE GOD'S HOUSE, AND OF ALL THAT YOU GIVE ME I WILL SURELY GIVE A TENTH TO YOU.' "
(GENESIS 28:20-22)

When this occurred, there was no priesthood in Jerusalem; it is presumed that Melchizedek was dead. There was no tabernacle of Moses - that would be three centuries later. There was no temple - that was still five hundred years away. So, what motivated Jacob to set up that memorial stone and make such a vow? Apparently, he understood the importance of where he was and the opportunity that had been provided to him to receive from God. In essence, his memorial stone designated this site as the place where God would give to man and where man would give to God.

When he returned twenty years later, he was indeed a wealthy man. True to his word, he was a giver. Ironically, he gave a gift to Esau - the same Esau who had determined to kill his brother. In fact, he demanded that Esau take a gift from him (Gen. 32:13, 18, 20 -21). The Hebrew word used to describe this gift is understood to be a "donation, tribute or sacrificial offering." Reading the account of what all he offered, one is impressed with the staggering size of the gift. By today's standards, Jacob's gift of livestock is estimated to be equivalent to about $50,000 in value. That is quite a bit when you consider that the gift was going to someone who had, from birth, been tempted to kill his brother for the birthright.

Yet, as I see it, the gift was indication that Jacob was able to rebuke the devourer. Moreover, God rebuked the death sentence that Esau had placed on him. In fact, by changing his name from Jacob (Hebrew *Ya'akov*) to Israel, God indicated to him that it was his destiny as Israel to rule over his enemies. In other words, when he was born - as *Ya'akov* - he had to protect his head from the heel of his enemy. As Israel, the role would be reversed - his heel would now be on the head of his enemies.

The Bible makes it clear that God rebuked the hate Esau had toward Jacob. He rebuked Esau's servants and prevented them from seizing Jacob's family. God rebuked anything and anybody that would prevent Jacob from taking the land of Canaan and fulfilling his destiny. So, we learn that when Jacob acted in obedience and offered unto the Lord, the devourer was rebuked. The relationship with his family was renewed, his immediate family was protected and his property was restored. He had "more than enough" (Gen. 33:11). The window - the gate of heaven - he had seen twenty years earlier remained open for him and his children.

KEEPING THE GATE OPEN

"DO YOU NOT KNOW THAT YOUR BODY IS THE TEMPLE OF THE HOLY SPIRIT WHO IS IN YOU, WHOM YOU HAVE FROM GOD, AND YOU ARE NOT YOUR OWN?"

(1 CORINTHIANS 6:19)

How can we keep the gate of heaven open in our life? First understand that you are the temple of the Holy Spirit. As such we are to keep the temple holy, that is, to keep unclean things from entering it. The way to attain this goal is to follow the Word in obedience; to pray consistently and earnestly; to fast and deny our flesh; and to give into God's house. Doing this will keep the "gate of heaven" open for you and your family. This is exactly how the Scripture lays it out for us.

Be led of the Spirit and walk in obedience.

"BUT SEEK FIRST THE KINGDOM OF GOD AND HIS RIGHTEOUSNESS, AND ALL THESE THINGS SHALL BE ADDED TO

YOU." (MATTHEW 6:33)

Bombard the heavens with our prayers.

"THE EFFECTIVE, FERVENT PRAYER OF A RIGHTEOUS MAN AVAILS MUCH." (JAMES 5:16)

Discipline ourselves by denying the flesh.

"AND THOSE WHO ARE CHRIST'S HAVE CRUCIFIED THE FLESH WITH ITS PASSIONS AND DESIRES."
(GALATIANS 5:24)

Demonstrate where our heart and treasures truly are - be a generous giver.

"BUT THIS I SAY: HE WHO SOWS SPARINGLY WILL ALSO REAP SPARINGLY, AND HE WHO SOWS BOUNTIFULLY WILL ALSO REAP BOUNTIFULLY." (2 CORINTHIANS 9:6)

When we do as God says - when He says - the result is blessing and prosperity - the gates of heaven are opened to us.

"BELOVED, I PRAY THAT YOU MAY PROSPER IN ALL THINGS AND BE IN HEALTH, JUST AS YOUR SOUL PROSPERS."
(3 JOHN 2)

There is one other point that I wish to make before moving on. Whether it pertains to financial giving or giving of ourselves, when we determine to promise God something we should count the costs first. Why? Because before God does something, He has already determined to remain committed to the decision. When He makes a vow, He keeps it. Consequently, He expects us to do the same.

The Law of Making and Breaking Vows

"When you make a vow to God, do not delay to pay it; For He has no pleasure in fools. Pay what you have vowed - better not to vow than to vow and not pay. Do not let your mouth cause your flesh to sin, nor say before the messenger of God that it was an error. Why should God be angry at your excuse and destroy the work of your hands?"

(Ecclesiastes 5:4-6)

Remember when a person's word was their bond? Remember when a handshake sealed a deal? Can you recall when a business went out of their way to keep their reputation in tact? Do you remember when you needed your car repaired and didn't worry about getting ripped off? How about the days when people stayed married despite hard times?

From a Biblical point of view, vows are critically important. So important, in fact, that God instilled specific consequences for breaking a vow. If you are experiencing lack in your marriage or lack in your finances, perhaps you should reflect on whether or not you have broken your vows.

What is a vow? It is a promise made in the form

of a prayer or petition. It is not claiming a promise but making a promise. When we claim God's promises, we are accepting His vows to us. That is something that most of us would have no trouble remembering or laying hold of. Yet, when we make a pledge to God, we oftentimes forget the promise almost as soon as we make it. Let's face it - breaking promises is something humans are good at. People continually break promises made to people because in many cases there are no repercussions. Yet, God takes our promises to Him much more seriously and especially when we make vows.

Many times, people will promise God things when in desperate situations. People facing tragedy and loss will vow to serve Him if "You will heal my child" or "put my family back together again." When the trouble passes and memories fade, so does the resolve to be faithful to the vow. However, whether the promises are made in desperation or not, God still considers them a vow. In God's eyes, when a promise is made, we need to be committed to keep the promise. Though we may forget, He does not.

In Biblical days, vows were accompanied with offerings, made with either livestock or money. This was to emphasize the importance of the vow and the person's commitment to keep his word. The Hebrew verb *nadar* (used 31 times in the Hebrew Scriptures) is used when "vowing" a gift to God. The noun form of the word (*neder*, used 60 times) is used when making a "promise" to God. The raw meaning of the word implies that something is being "projected forward."

Thus, when a vow is made, it is understood that something being affirmed now is meant to affect something in the future. If we go back on our vow, then what we "projected forward" potentially falls apart.

A related word used in Scripture is *asar*. This is commonly interpreted as a "bond" (as in Numbers 30:4-11). It signifies a promise that "binds" two people together. The root meaning, "to hitch or yoke together" conveys the idea of two animals (or people) tied to one another for a common task or goal. Marriage is an example of this type of bond or vow whereas tithing is an example of the word *neder*.

To Swear An Oath

"Dwell in this land, and I will be with you and bless you; for to you and your descendants I give all these lands, and I will perform the oath which I swore to Abraham your father." (Genesis 26:3)

Seven is a powerful number in the Scripture. The value seven continually shows up in the Bible - 372 times to be exact. The first occurrence is in the days of Creation - the seventh day being the day of rest, the Sabbath. Other examples of the occurrence of seven in Scripture are listed here.

❖ Noah was given seven days warning before going into the ark (Gen. 7:4).

- ❖ The dove sent from the ark returned after seven days (Gen. 8:10).
- ❖ After seven days the dove sent a second time but never returned (Gen. 8:12).
- ❖ Abraham offered seven lambs as a sign of covenant between him and Abimelech (Gen. 21:28).
- ❖ Jacob served Laban for two terms of seven years each (Gen. 29).
- ❖ Laban pursued Jacob seven days before catching up to him (Gen. 31:23).
- ❖ Jacob bowed seven times before Esau (Gen. 33:3).
- ❖ Egypt enjoyed seven years of plenty (Gen. 41).
- ❖ The world endured seven years of famine (Gen. 41).
- ❖ Jacob's death was mourned for seven days (Gen. 50:10).
- ❖ The Nile River was turned to blood for seven days (Ex. 8:25).
- ❖ The seven feasts of Israel (Lev. 23)

There are many other instances where seven appears in Scripture. In fact, it is so prevalent that seven is considered the number of completion and thus, anything tied to this value is considered "complete" or "done." Consequently, the number seven is tied to the judgment of God. There is a seven-year tribulation, a book with seven seals, seven vial judgments, seven trumpet judgments. He even said that He would punish Israel for breaking the covenant, "seven times more."

"Then, if you walk contrary to Me, and are not willing to obey Me, I will bring on you seven times more plagues, according to your sins. I will also send wild beasts among you, which shall rob you of your children, destroy your livestock, and make you few in number; and your highways shall be desolate. And if by these things you are not reformed by Me, but walk contrary to Me, then I also will walk contrary to you, and I will punish you yet seven times for your sins." (Leviticus 26:21-24)

The Hebrew root word for seven is *sheva*. The root of this word is *shaba* and is translated as "swear" or "swore" as in an oath. The root meaning is literally to "submit to God," or "complete." This concept of this word is obviously connected to the number seven, which hints at completion. *Strong's Exhaustive Concordance* goes so far as to define *shaba* as meaning "to seven oneself," because to do so - to swear an oath - is likened unto when God makes an oath, as in the above passage. Consequently from a Biblical perspective,"to swear" an oath is akin to swearing by what is holy. It is a serious matter. Not surprisingly, the Hebrew word for "oath" also has as its root the word *shaba*.

Two Levels of Vows

An unconditional vow is one in which you have bound yourself with an oath without expecting anything in return. For instance:

"IF A MAN MAKES A VOW TO THE LORD, OR SWEARS AN OATH TO BIND HIMSELF BY SOME AGREEMENT, HE SHALL NOT BREAK HIS WORD; HE SHALL DO ACCORDING TO ALL THAT PROCEEDS OUT OF HIS MOUTH." (NUMBERS 30:2)

An example of a conditional vow is like the one I referred to earlier that Jacob made when he was in need of Divine protection and promised to repay the LORD in return for His assistance. There is obviously power in such a vow to God, for what Jacob promised came true. However, before making such a vow, one needs to consider that the vow must be based on the truth of Scripture. It cannot go outside the parameters of the covenant. The vow must always be in sync with promises God has already made. Most importantly, when you make a vow it should always be predicated on you being obedient to Him. If you do that, He will be with you.

In this particular instance, Jacob isn't asking for anything that isn't already established before he uttered those words. In other words, we can already see in the text that God intended to protect him from Esau because He had already done so in Rebekah's womb and while Jacob was being born (Gen. 25). My friend Bill Cloud has pointed out that the reason

Jacob's hand was on Esau's heel was not in order to supplant Esau's birthright, but to keep Esau's heel from crushing his head. Now, how would a child instinctively know to do such a thing unless God was already protecting him?

When Jacob promised to give tithes to the Lord, he is faithfully following in the footsteps of his righteous grandfather, Abraham, who tithed to Melchizedek (Gen. 14:20, Heb. 7:1-2). He does this to offer what will be a sign or token of the vow he has made. In other words, it becomes a sign of the covenant between him and God. Yet, Jacob knows that to do so is not cost, but gain. To do so - to walk in obedience - is to be blessed and walk in abundant life.

While vows made to God are potentially powerful, vows made to men can be just as powerful but in a destructive way. What I mean by this is when we make a vow to a church or a religious system and not necessarily to God, then our spiritual walk is at risk of being defined by men instead of God's Word.

For instance, when I was growing up in the Pentecostal church there were certain criteria that must be met before one could join the congregation. Excessive jewelry, going to the movies, swimming with the opposite sex among other things were all considered taboo. Thousands promised to abandon such things because they thought they were appropriate. As time passed, the strict prohibition on certain teachings were relaxed, in part, because it was believed these teachings had been the result of men's opinions. When this change came about, some of the older saints became confused and were convinced that the church was "breaking a vow" made before God.

There are other churches (i.e. the Catholic Church) who have had similar experiences when Church teaching has changed. The issue is this: when the people vowed to do something or to abstain from something, were they making a vow before God or before man? Was their vow made for spiritual purposes or for good standing with a religious system? In other words, do people at times make vows based on spiritual ignorance and insufficient Biblical knowledge? Such vows made lead to disappointment and, in some cases, disillusionment.

Prior to making a vow, we should think about what we are considering because we should be committed to seeing it through. I have made vows to God that I have been able to keep because I meditated upon the significance of what I was doing. I vowed that I would be above reproach when it came to handling money and using the assets of the ministry. When we sell teaching resources, the revenues all go back into the ministry. We do not sell our mailing list to businesses. We don't send out letters to our donors each month soliciting donations.

These are vows I made at the outset and have kept for almost thirty years and as a result, God has blessed the ministry for it. And so, if we have made vows flippantly and have gone back on those vows, it is important that we repent of our haste and our unfaithfulness to that vow.

In the season of *teshuvah* - days when decisions are made that potentially determine future blessing - it is important to be committed to our decisions. When Jacob established his memorial at Bethel, he did so with the understanding that he was under an open window. He knew that he was in a "season" where the eyes and ears of heaven were focused upon him. He set up his memorial and vowed unto the Lord. He kept his word and so did God.

Chapter Six

A TIME
OF RELEASE

"AND WHENEVER YOU STAND PRAYING, IF YOU HAVE ANYTHING AGAINST ANYONE, FORGIVE HIM, THAT YOUR FATHER IN HEAVEN MAY ALSO FORGIVE YOU YOUR TRESPASSES." (MARK 11:25)

What is *teshuvah* - repentance? It is much more than saying, "I'm sorry." Of course, saying "I'm sorry" is a start, but if we are truly repentant then we are going to turn back to God with all of our heart, soul and strength (Deut. 6:5). True repentance will change our way of thinking, because how we think determines what we do. True repentance will change our attitude toward God, His ways and our fellow man. In short, repentance will expose and purge what has been in our heart before we decided to "turn."

Unfortunately, many people stop short of true repentance and, oftentimes, it is due to the fact that they have a hard time forgiving someone else of something that person did to injure them. In some cases, they can't seem to forgive themselves of things they have done. So many people have to grapple these issues and, as we see from the Scripture, if we do not overcome this unforgiveness, our relationship with God is going to be inhibited. And so, during the season of *teshuvah* it is just as important to forgive others their trespasses even as we are turning back to God and seeking His forgiveness and His blessing.

I believe there is a simple yet powerful four part process to experiencing freedom from unforgiveness, guilt and condemnation. First, **you must trace it**. What is the root cause of your conflict? Many times individuals evade digging deep into their own heart and deal with difficulty on a surface level. They may say, "My wife and I do not get along." What is the root cause of the conflict? Is it rebellion, lack of communication?

If your husband is not interested in repenting of his sins and turning to Christ, what is the main hindrance? Is he bound by addictions, by alcohol, by pornography? These fleshly sins attach themselves and drain the life and spiritual reasoning from people just like a leech. This type of situation hinders them and impedes a life of freedom in Christ.

After discovering the root of the problem, **you must face it**. You cannot enjoy the future living in the past, and God does not consult your past to determine your destiny. Spiritual progress becomes as stagnant as a swamp in a dry spell when people continually blame everyone else for the condition they are in. You can never be delivered from bondage as long as you justify your condition by blaming others. Only by admitting, "I am a sinner. I need your help. I need God's power to change my life" can the Word of God go into motion on your behalf.

Third, **you must erase it**. Removing the unforgiveness and strife from your heart comes by confessing before God that you hold grudges, bitterness and unforgiveness within you. You must see that your mind has become a mental prison, and you have captured individuals and are holding them hostage because you hate how they treated you. Erasing the conflict raging in your heart does not come by, "mind over matter," or simply repeating, "I believe it is gone." You have to get rid of it.

True repentance means that you are willing to tell God that you regret your action and you desire His power to forgive and forget those who have offended you. After this, then the work of the Holy Spirit is to bring about the "regeneration" (Titus 3:5). The Greek word translated as "regeneration" in Titus 3:5 means, "a spiritual rebirth," or a "spiritual renovation." It is like an old house infested with dust, cobwebs and dead insects in every corner. The house needs a thorough house cleaning complete with new paint and wallpaper. Multitudes of people have experienced the freedom and release when God's Spirit set them free from the unhealthy conditions of their past. Only He can break through the hatred that people have felt toward those who mistreated them. True repentance leads to true refreshing and restoration (Acts 3:19).

Finally, **you must replace** the empty places in your heart and spirit with the Word of God and the power of the Holy Spirit. Repentance toward God and toward our fellow man is so important, because the offenses created by words and misunderstandings keep myriads of people from attending a local congregation and cause many an individual to remain spiritually defeated. Through the years I have met older people who will not go to church because of an incident which occurred many years ago, involving the elders, deacons, choir or a pastor. They will rehash something that occurred long ago and continually wallow in their personal opinions. Some of them are proud that they have not stepped foot in a church since that time. Religion can't do anything for these people - only the Word of God can replace such an empty spot.

FORTY YEARS OF OFFENSE

My father and his brother Morgan were converted in November of 1949. In the fall of 1950, Dad and Morgan attended a revival at the Church of God in Christ in Yukon, WV. At one point Morgan walked out to go to the men's room. At that time the pastor's son, who was away from God and had been drinking, stood up with a pistol in his hand and pointed it toward the altar. The young man yelled, "These old Holy Rollers always talk about heaven. Let's see who wants to get there."

About that time, Morgan returned to the service, saw the gun and grabbed the man's hand and pointed the gun back into the man's stomach. As someone went for the police, Morgan restrained the boy. Instead of rebuking his son, the pastor stood by silent as his drunk son threatened Morgan. Instead of dealing with his son, the pastor then rebuked Morgan for dealing so harshly with his son.

The following night the same man was drunk again and this time he brought a knife to the church. He proceeded to provoke Morgan and tried to coax him into a fight. Instead of having the boy arrested, the pastor sympathized with his son. Because the pastor did not take a stand with Morgan - the one who was protecting the people - Morgan left the church and refused to go back. As a result Morgan went into a spiritual decline and stayed that way for over forty years. This one incident brought such an offense that he was unable and unwilling to serve the Lord.

Forty years later Morgan and a friend were driving through McDowell County, WV and stopped at a restaurant-bar. As they were sipping on a coke, Morgan heard a male voice behind him saying, "Oh Lord. Morgan Ball, is that you?" When Morgan turned, he recognized the man who forty years before tried to pick a fight with him in church. Morgan thought the old fellow was still wanting to start a fight. Morgan stood and went toward the fellow ready to "knock his teeth out." When he approached the man, instead of fighting, the fellow stuck out his hand and said, "Morgan. I'm sorry for what happened years ago. I have been tormented all of these years because I heard you had quit church. I didn't know if you were still living or not."

Morgan was so touched that his heart was softened. Dad told him, "Morgan. I told you through the years that God would take care of this. All of these years this man was living under condemnation and was afraid you had died before he could apologize to you." He said, "Morgan. You allowed the enemy to defeat you for forty years and didn't know how the fellow who mistreated you was tormented during those same forty years."

FREEDOM FROM TEMPTATION

While reading the Lord's Prayer I noticed how freedom from temptation is linked to your willingness to forgive others.

"IN THIS MANNER, THEREFORE, PRAY: OUR FATHER IN HEAVEN, HALLOWED BE YOUR NAME. YOUR KINGDOM COME. YOUR WILL BE DONE ON EARTH AS IT IS IN HEAVEN. GIVE US THIS DAY OUR DAILY BREAD AND FORGIVE US OUR DEBTS, AS WE FORGIVE OUR DEBTORS. AND DO NOT LEAD US INTO TEMPTATION, BUT DELIVER US FROM THE EVIL ONE. FOR YOURS IS THE KINGDOM AND THE POWER AND THE GLORY FOREVER. AMEN." (MATTHEW 6:9-13)

As we are willing to forgive others, our own spiritual freedom can help us avoid the temptations of the enemy. I recall a well-known minster who appeared on world wide television calling a fellow minister who had fallen into a sin of immorality, "a cancer in the Body of Christ." My spirit was so grieved to see a minister crush a fallen brother deeper into the ground. Two years later this minister was caught with a prostitute not far from his ministry headquarters. He later said that he had prayed and prayed but was unable to get freedom from his struggle. From a Biblical perspective I can tell you why he prayed and prayed without results. Jesus taught that, if you do not forgive your brother his trespasses, neither would your heavenly Father forgive your of your trespasses.

"FOR IF YOU FORGIVE MEN THEIR TRESPASSES, YOUR HEAVENLY FATHER WILL ALSO FORGIVE YOU. BUT IF YOU DO NOT FORGIVE MEN THEIR TRESPASSES, NEITHER WILL YOUR FATHER FORGIVE YOUR TRESPASSES."

(MATTHEW 6:14-15).

Because of his unforgiving attitude toward another brother, this minister not only opened himself up to continual temptation, but he was unable to escape the consequences of his own weakness. This was due, at least in part, to the grudge he held against another person.

Forgiveness is so important that Christ did not expire on the cross until He cried out, "Father forgive them, for they know not what they do" (Lk. 23:34). As the first martyr in the church, Stephen also prayed for his enemies even as he was being stoned to death, saying, "Lay not this sin to their charge" (Acts 7:60). The Apostle Peter informs us that strife among two believers, including a husband and wife, can actually hinder prayers from being answered.

"HUSBANDS, LIKEWISE, DWELL WITH THEM WITH UNDERSTANDING, GIVING HONOR TO THE WIFE, AS TO THE WEAKER VESSEL, AND AS BEING HEIRS TOGETHER OF THE GRACE OF LIFE, THAT YOUR PRAYERS MAY NOT BE HINDERED." (1 PETER 3:7)

Another area that unforgiveness affects people is finances. For years I ministered in rural churches where believers had attended for years. When finances were discussed, some would comment, "I have given money to the church for years and I have never experienced a financial breakthrough that these preachers are always talking about." After spending some time hearing these same people complaining, criticizing the church and the minister and talking about others in a negative way, I knew why they were restrained financially, not to mention why they were always sick and tired. God refuses to bless anyone who has offense toward another believer.

"THEREFORE IF YOU BRING YOUR GIFT TO THE ALTAR, AND THERE REMEMBER THAT YOUR BROTHER HAS SOMETHING AGAINST YOU, LEAVE YOUR GIFT THERE BEFORE THE ALTAR, AND GO YOUR WAY. FIRST BE RECONCILED TO YOUR BROTHER, AND THEN COME AND OFFER YOUR GIFT." (MATTHEW 5:23-24)

In the ministry of Jesus, healing and forgiveness of sins went hand in hand. Often, Jesus would first address the sin issue before manifesting the healing. In Mark 2:9 He said, "Your sins are forgiven you" before He healed the sick man of his palsy. After curing a lame man, Jesus said, "Go and sin no more least a worse thing come upon you" (Jn. 5:14). When a person forgives others, their spirit is then open to receive their own forgiveness from God and the consequent blessing.

Unforgiveness not only hinders your prayer and stops the flow of financial blessing, but can also nullify your "spiritual warfare." Matthew 7:14-15 teaches that God is not under any obligation to hear the prayer of a believer who is not walking in obedience to God's Word. Since God is not obligated to hear your prayer, then Satan is not under any spiritual or legal obligation to obey your rebuke.

I have said it this way: "If God is not hearing your prayers then Satan is not listening to your warfare." You can bind the devil, rebuke the enemy and come against the powers of darkness. However, if in your heart there is strife, bitterness and unforgiveness, then your prayers and rebuke are simply spiritual gymnastics with little or no results. The issue of forgiveness may be the primary reason why so many Christians are falling short of God's blessing in their lives. Is this describing you? Don't wait until tomorrow; do something about it today.

My Personal Teshuvah

In late summer 2005, I was teaching about *Teshuvah* on our weekly television program, *Manna-Fest*. During one particular program I emphasized the importance of searching your heart to ensure that there was no one that you have any ought against, even if your inner search went back many years. During the time I recalled an incident which had occurred over twenty-five years ago. It involved the pastor of a local church where I had ministered.

Following an extended revival, the enemy arose and caused a great division in the church. Some had blamed me, some blamed the pastor and others discerned it was a sly attack from the Adversary. In short, I thought I had forgiven everyone involved in the issue, when I began to think about the pastor's wife. I was impressed to write her a personal letter and ask forgiveness for past events. I personally held nothing against the woman but felt it would bring a complete healing and closure to the matter. The problem was, I did not have her address and did not know where she was living.

The following day I was in a local book store and met a friend who pastored a church in Virginia. We had not seen one another in many, many years. Yet, it just so happened that this friend knew the pastor and his wife - the one I wished to write. I began to ask about the older minister's wife and he said, "She attends my church." I told him I desired to write her a letter. He gave me her address.

I spent several hours carefully wording a four page letter that explained in detail the events of that time, and how I was sorry for any misunderstanding. I placed the letter in overnight mail and sensed a strong peace of God come over me. I knew that *teshuvah* was not only a time of personal repentance but a time to forgive and release others.

The following day I received a totally unexpected phone call from a book company who was offering to print and distribute our books not only in North America but throughout the world. A few weeks later, I was ministering at our Main Event Campmeeting in Dalton, GA. The thirtieth day of *teshuvah* concluded during the meeting we held on *Rosh Hashanah* - the Feast of Trumpets. That night, a businessman handed me the largest check the ministry had ever received. The check was to assist us in the building of our International Ministry Center. I truly believe these unexpected blessings were a result of God honoring His Word when I sought to be obedient.

Now please hear me on this - we should not wait for any particular time, for "today is the day of salvation." Nevertheless, we need to understand that God has determined that there are "appointed times." And so just as a farmer plants the seed in the early spring for a harvest at the appointed time, we too plant our prayers and our offerings in the proper season expecting there to be a harvest when we most need it. When we plant that seed, make sure that there is nothing hidden in our heart that would hinder that seed from bringing forth fruit. What we do during the season of *teshuvah* and how we do it will affect the results we anticipate for the future.

IN CONCLUSION

In this book I have attempted to show that God truly has ordained certain seasons and cycles - His appointed times. I have also sought to demonstrate that what we do during these appointed times can determine how our immediate and long-term future is affected. There is definitely something to the idea that God teaches us through these special seasons and cycles.

During these last three decades of ministry I have observed that the greatest attacks seem to come in the spring, specifically between Passover and Pentecost. The greatest breakthroughs have come during the summer months, and in particular the month of August. Of course, this is approximately the time when the forty days of *teshuvah* begin. In my life and in my ministry, the greatest revivals have come in the fall months. The greatest financial breakthroughs seem to always occur in a season beginning in late summer and the early to mid fall - in other words, from the beginning of the days of *teshuvah* until the end of the final "appointed times."

You might think this to be coincidental or maybe you are tempted to think this is all just for good reading. I assure you that I am completely convinced that God moves in unique and singular ways during these times that He has designated as "appointed."

Because I am so convinced, I want to pass this information along to you and hope that you too will be motivated, as I have been, to learn of God's special seasons. Moreover, I want God's people to respond as God would have us to during these appointed times. Why? So that His purposes for the Kingdom and for us as individuals would be accomplished. If you want to experience a season of refreshing, a season of restoration and a time of release, then dedicate yourself to a time of repentance - God's way.

Perhaps you are reading this at a time when the forty days of *teshuvah* (1st of *Elul* through the Day of Atonement) are soon approaching. If so, I challenge you to respond appropriately during this special time. If you are reading this at a time of year when the season is far away, do not delay, but apply the principles you have learned in this book and make changes in your life **today**! Every day, regardless of a calendar date, is the right season to turn back to God. Every day is the proper time to experience spiritual renewal. For you see, Judgment Day is coming; the shofar has sounded and today is the day to act! Today can be your day of repentance, of refreshing and complete restoration. Amen.

The Days of Teshuvah and Accompanying Feast Days for the Next Ten Years

Hebrew Year / Gregorian Year

Please note that all these holy days begin on the evening prior to the date listed.

5766-5767 / 2006

1 Elul 5766 (1st day of Teshuvah) - August 25, 2006
1 Tishri 5767 (Rosh Hashana) - September 23, 2006
10 Tishri 5767 (Yom Kippur) - October 2, 2006
15 Tishri 5767 (1st day of Sukkot) - October 7, 2006
22 Tishri 5767 (Shemini Atzeret) - October 14, 2006

5767-5768 / 2007

1 Elul 5767 (1st day of Teshuvah) - August 15, 2007
1 Tishri 5768 (Rosh Hashana) - September 13, 2007
10 Tishri 5768 (Yom Kippur) - September 22, 2007
15 Tishri 5768 (1st day of Sukkot) - September 27, 2007
22 Tishri 5768 (Shemini Atzeret) - October 4, 2007

5768-5769 / 2008

1 Elul 5768 (1st day of Teshuvah) - September 1, 2008
1 Tishri 5769 (Rosh Hashana) - September 30, 2008
10 Tishri 5769 (Yom Kippur) - October 9, 2008
15 Tishri 5769 (1st day of Sukkot) - October 14, 2008
22 Tishri 5769 (Shemini Atzeret) - October 21, 2008

5769-5770 / 2009

1 Elul 5769 (1st day of Teshuvah) - August 21, 2009
1 Tishri 5770 (Rosh Hashana) - September 19, 2009
10 Tishri 5770 (Yom Kippur) - September 28, 2009
15 Tishri 5770 (1st day of Sukkot) - October 3, 2009
22 Tishri 5770 (Shemini Atzeret) - October 10, 2009

5770-5771 / 2010

1 Elul 5770 (1st day of Teshuvah) - August 11, 2010
1 Tishri 5771 (Rosh Hashana) - September 9, 2010
10 Tishri 5771 (Yom Kippur) - September 18, 2010

15 Tishri 5771 (1st day of Sukkot) - September 23, 2010
22 Tishri 5771 (Shemini Atzeret) - September 30, 2010

5771-5772 / 2011
1 Elul 5771 (1st day of Teshuvah) - August 31, 2011
1 Tishri 5772 (Rosh Hashana) - September 29, 2011
10 Tishri 5772 (Yom Kippur) - October 8, 2011
15 Tishri 5772 (1st day of Sukkot) - October 13, 2011
22 Tishri 5772 (Shemini Atzeret) - October 20, 2011

5772-5773 / 2012
1 Elul 5772 (1st day of Teshuvah) - August 19, 2012
1 Tishri 5773 (Rosh Hashana) - September 17, 2012
10 Tishri 5773 (Yom Kippur) - September 26, 2012
15 Tishri 5773 (1st day of Sukkot) - October 1, 2012
22 Tishri 5773 (Shemini Atzeret) - October 8, 2012

5773-5774 / 2013
1 Elul 5773 (1st day of Teshuvah) - August 7, 2013
1 Tishri 5774 (Rosh Hashana) - September 5, 2013
10 Tishri 5774 (Yom Kippur) - September 14, 2013
15 Tishri 5774 (1st day of Sukkot) - September 19, 2013
22 Tishri 5774 (Shemini Atzeret) - September 26, 2013

5774-5775 / 2014
1 Elul 5774 (1st day of Teshuvah) - August 27, 2014
1 Tishri 5775 (Rosh Hashana) - September 25, 2014
10 Tishri 5775 (Yom Kippur) - October 4, 2014
15 Tishri 5775 (1st day of Sukkot) - October 9, 2014
22 Tishri 5775 (Shemini Atzeret) - October 16, 2014

5775-5776 / 2015
1 Elul 5775 (1st day of Teshuvah) - August 16, 2015
1 Tishri 5776 (Rosh Hashana) - September 14, 2015
10 Tishri 5776 (Yom Kippur) - September 23, 2015
15 Tishri 5776 (1st day of Sukkot) - September 28, 2015
22 Tishri 5776 (Shemini Atzeret) - October 5, 2015

GLOSSARY OF HEBREW TERMS

General Terms
chadash/chadashah - "renewed"
chodesh - "month"
hag - "holy day, festival"
Mishnah - rabbinical commentary on the Hebrew scriptures.
moedim - "appointed times"
rosh - "head"
shuv - "turn back"
teshuvah - "repentance"
yom - "day"

Times of Year
Av - Hebrew month occurring in Jul./Aug.
Aviv - "springtime" - Hebrew month occurring in Mar./Apr.
Elul - Hebrew month typically occurring in Aug./early Sept.
Nisan - another name for the Hebrew month Aviv.
Tishri - Hebrew month occurring in Sept./Oct.

Special Days
Pesach - "Passover"
Rosh Chodesh - "head (beginning) of the month"
Rosh ha Shana - "head (beginning) of the year"
Shabbat - "Sabbath"
Shavuot - "weeks" - Feast of Weeks (Pentecost).
Shemini Atzeret - "Eighth Day" - final day of Sukkot.
Simchat Torah - "Rejoicing in the Torah"
Sukkot - "booths" - Feast of Booths (Tabernacles)
Yom Kippur - "Day of Atonement"
Yom Teruah - "Day of blowing (trumpets)" Feast of Trumpets